Notes on the Science of Picture-making

i

NOTES ON THE SCIENCE OF
PICTURE-MAKING
C. J. HOLMES

"Innocence"
from a medal by Pisanello

NOTES ON THE SCIENCE OF
PICTURE-MAKING

BY

(Sir) Charles John HOLMES

DIRECTOR OF THE NATIONAL GALLERY
SOMETIME SLADE PROFESSOR OF FINE ART IN THE
UNIVERSITY OF OXFORD

LONDON
CHATTO & WINDUS
MCMXX

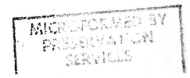

Fourth Edition

Printed in Great Britain by Butler & Tanner,
Frome and London

TO

C. S. R , L. B.

R. E. F., A. J. B.

PREFACE TO THE FOURTH EDITION

ON looking over these old lectures I notice many details which I should now be inclined to alter or to express differently. During the last decade the resources of painting, like those of politics, have been tested to breaking point, and we shall never be able to regard art with quite the same eye as before. But a cool survey of this æsthetic battlefield shows that, in spite of all the din and debris of conflict, the old landmarks stand just where they did. One or two may be rather less prominent : that is all.

For example, in these pages Repose is mentioned as one of the characteristics of all great art. So it remains, but modern taste would certainly give it less importance than Vitality, especially in questions of colour. Colour indeed is being studied as it has seldom or never been studied before. Persian Miniatures, oriental Carpets, with the art products of Japan and China, have contributed largely to this study, while in the special field of painting men like Gauguin, Van Gogh and Cézanne have broken new ground for controversy or enjoyment. So potent indeed have been these influences that for those who feel them strongly, much of the painting which has passed muster for centuries ceases to have any living interest.

It is difficult, for instance, to believe that the typical brownish " Old Master " will ever again excite genuine enthusiasm in any educated lover of art. Even among the great ones of the earth a similar distinction may some day be drawn, and a Rubens with all his fire and brilliancy of handling will stimulate us less than some vivid primitive, while Filippo Lippi will seem tame and sophisticated in the presence of Angelico. Indeed Angelico, Uccello, Piero della Francesca and the young Michelangelo seem now to hold their own, even with the great Venetians, in the matter of colour as well as in design. This change is no mere momentary fashion. In the matter of design it is doubtless a natural reaction from the experimental violence, naïveness, or anarchy of the modern schools, which will in time yield or lead to other styles ; but in the matter of colour it is hard to imagine any reversion to darkness and dullness. The untaught collector will, of course, go on buying dingy paintings, as he goes on buying drawings by Copley Fielding or Birket Foster, and will have the usual following of living mediocrities to applaud him ; but the demand for such things whether old or modern is a matter of business and has no connexion with or interest for the creative artist.

So far as the classification adopted in this book is concerned, the recent innovations may be treated under the heads of Symbol, of Colour and of Material. Unity of Symbol has been carried to its extreme limit by the reduction of all objects to geometrical terms by the

Cubists. Their products thus attained undeniable unity of a kind, and sometimes expressed volume and mass with a certain success : but the unity and the success were of the limited order which may be achieved with a child's box of bricks, and have proved too limited in their range of expression to retain interest even for those who, like Picasso, led the way in exploring. On purely decorative work, and on textiles, Cubism may leave its mark, for it necessitates the repetition of similar forms and similar tones—the essential elements of decorative rhythm, but it is unlikely that it will play any but a subordinate part in the making of pictures.

The treatment of contour has been extended in similar fashion from simplification to distortion, with results which are variously estimated. Simplification is essential to artistic expressiveness, but distortion is a dangerous tool. Where it is the result of swift handling and vehement feeling as in an emphatic sketch by Rembrandt or Daumier, it may be magnificent ; it may not be incongruous in some fierce rhythmic invention of Greco, of William Blake or of Van Gogh ; it is the weapon, *par excellence*, of all great satirists and caricaturists. To extend its function beyond these clearly defined provinces, to employ it deliberately as a means of avoiding the difficulties of plain narrative, is a mistake. Every variation from natural form must, if we are to avoid incongruity, be accompanied by an equivalent variation from natural colour. If form is simplified, colour must be simplified also : if form is distorted, the colour change must be equally drastic (p. 43). Here indeed we have a useful touchstone for much modern painting. In the best work of Gaugain and Van Gogh and in the Still-life pieces of Cézanne, this correspondence is maintained. Where contours are simplified, colour is simplified ; where colour is forced to an extreme pitch, design and contour are handled with equal daring. Failure begins where form is distorted, while the colour remains in some degree naturalistic.

And colour has assumed, quite rightly, so much importance, that to secure it in its greatest possible breadth and intensity, some corresponding simplification and concentration of design is seen to be essential. To attain that simplicity and that concentration without sacrificing the plastic and expressive qualities of fine draughtsmanship, is the task of the modern artist. Lowness of relief will do much. Much too will depend on the colouring of the shadows. It is recognized now that one of the secrets of the finest and most brilliant colouring, is not to lay stress on the colour of the lights, but to reserve the most intense tones of colour for the half-lights or the shadows. If the shadows be full of colour, the lights may be almost colourless. Such painting may lack some of those qualities of recession and relief which we have been accustomed to admire in the painting of the seventeenth and eighteenth centuries, but the gain in general attractiveness of aspect, and in decorative quality, will far more than outweigh the loss.

This advance, however, will not become general until we become more sensitive to material, and more strenuous in learning its proper treatment, than most painters at present seem to be. Years ago in these pages the various methods of handling oil paint were discussed, and a general preference expressed for using thin or comparatively thin pigment. Time has turned that preference into a conviction. The thick rough pigment so generally employed to-day by painters of very different schools and aims, not only makes real delicacy of handling, and therewith delicacy of expression, exceedingly difficult, but it also involves a real risk to all fine tone and colour. The oil contained in the thick masses of paint must almost inevitably rise in time to the surface and form that leathery film which already dulls and disfigures so many capable pictures produced during the last two decades. The more delicate and subtle a tone, the more fatal this depreciation becomes, and the more easily is it incurred. If therefore we are to have a school of colour, we must have a style of painting which suits colour. Tempera as a foundation was successful in the past. The more direct and impatient worker of to-day will probably continue to call for oil painting. If so, he will be wise to paint as thinly as he can, dispensing, so far as possible, with oil as a medium. Holbein and Ingres in portraiture, in figure painting Michelangelo and Bronzino, not to mention earlier masters, will point the way at Trafalgar Square. For the landscape of the future there are no such accessible signposts, and we can only try to imagine how Piero della Francesca, or Korin, or any other mighty man we admire, would have painted " Mousehold Heath."

Chiaroscuro, speaking generally, is out of favour,

but the objection does not apply to the greatest Chiaro
scurist of all. Rembrandt stands apart and alone.
His method of painting is appropriate only to his own
range of thought and his own personal temper, except,
perhaps, in the field of portraiture, where, as Leonardo
da Vinci found out long before, a full range of tone from
deep dark to full light, is valuable, if not essential, for
profound psychological analysis. Rembrandt's relation
to the Masters of Colour I have tried to explain elsewhere,* but I may repeat briefly in this place a definite
conclusion to which the prolonged study and comparison
of the various schools at Trafalgar Square has brought
me.

It is this. That only the supreme painters can make
any free use of chiaroscuro without immediately suffering for it. The shadows of oil-painting never get
lighter, and often get very much darker. Mastic varnish,
too, turns a rich brown in the course of time, gilding the
light parts of a picture but adding still further to the
gloom of the shadows. This varnish, it is true, can
easily be removed, and the lights will then flash out
with their pristine freshness, but the shadows are past
remedy, and will remain impenetrably black. If then
we wish to paint for eternity, as we ought to wish, we
must be careful to treat our half tones as the colourist
treats them, to keep them comparatively pale, and yet
full of colour, from which the notes of deep shadow or
black which we use for accent shall stand out sharply.
" Let your white be precious and your black conspicu-

* *Notes on the Art of Rembrandt.* London, Chatto and
Windus. 1911.

ous " was one of Ruskin's wisest maxims. But the great fact is that the schools of colour seem to stand the test of time, while the schools of chiaroscuro do not, except in the case of a few very great men, whose psychological and technical gifts make us overlook the gloomy outward appearance of their pictures. Van Eyck and Bruegel De Hooch and Vermeer prove that the Flemish and Dutch oil methods may be used with no loss of brightness where colour and design and fine workmanship are primary aims. It is only when artists become attracted by the fatal fascination of playing about with brown shadows, a royal road to the facile picturesque, that trouble begins. Yet the modern practice of painting thickly and roughly will prove in time hardly less fatal, for reasons I have mentioned elsewhere. In short, the single chance of escape, as it seems to me, is to attempt to be a colourist, to fill shadows with definite colour (the richer the better), to model in low relief, to use black and white only or chiefly as accents, and to paint cleanly, broadly, and thinly. Some effects perhaps cannot be obtained quite on those terms : but if we keep those terms in mind, we may at least make a better bargain with Fortune than if we had gone to work haphazard.

C. J. H.

October 1919.

CONTENTS

PART I

EMPHASIS OF DESIGN

PART II

EMPHASIS OF MATERIALS

PART III

EMPHASIS OF CHARACTER

SUMMARY

INTRODUCTION

THE blunders which we continually make in our estimates of contemporary painting, and the incessant squabbles between painters themselves, do not argue that art criticism so far has been of much practical use, either to the world in general, or to the limited class of persons who might be expected to read it. So far as the general public is concerned, the æsthetic philosopher may be absolved for his non-success. If he has failed to teach it the principles of reason, judgment and good taste, no other kind of philosopher has been much more successful. Yet when we come to the restricted class of educated persons, who have been closely connected with the Fine Arts in some capacity or other, the æsthetic philosopher has been more conspicuously ineffective. The musician and the man of letters no longer dispute except over trifles, but artists are still at open war over what would seem to be the very rudiments of taste: School fights with School and Society with Society. The man who, for one section of the art world, is a consummate genius, seems in all verity to another section to be a charlatan and a coxcomb.

Fierce though the conflicts may occasionally be that rage in the kindred domain of music and literature, we find there a general thread of logical agreement uniting all intelligent persons, except upon minor details ; just as in the world of science men have ceased to argue that the world is flat, or that Archbishop Ussher's chronology is trustworthy, let us say, beyond B.C. 4000. Where they still contest they contest only such abstruse, though fundamental, problems as the digestion of the phagocyte, or the disposition of positive and negative electrons in the atom.

In æsthetics we seem to be still almost as far from this unity as were men of science three centuries ago. A few giant reputations alone rise permanently above the cloudy sea of controversy, and even their summits now and then are touched by stray wisps of prejudice. Around the rest the misty tide of criticism continues to ebb and flow, now overwhelming some peak that for long years basked in the sun of popularity, now uncovering some other mountain mass hitherto shrouded in oblivion.

In spite of all the mighty names connected in one way or another with the criticism of the fine arts, we have still no fixed standard for passing judgment on pictures already existing ; much less such a system of training the intelligence as will save us from making gross blunders as to future productions. We can make a sort of system, perhaps, for judging one particular class of work, for Florentine painting of the Renaissance, or for Hellenic sculpture, but these touchstones fail us absolutely when we try them upon a Claude Monet or a Monticelli.

Æsthetic critics, then, one and all have failed in the chief part of their business; and why? To answer is not easy, but I believe the fault lies at the door of those who have led men's thoughts away from the practical side of the arts to dream over enticing abstract terms such as Truth and Beauty. Philosophers have concerned themselves with an ideal of perfect beauty as the foundation of artistic success. Men of letters,* if thoughtfully minded, have usually followed the philosophers, trying all the while to reconcile the abstract philosophic ideal with "Truth to Nature." Painters have not written so much as we could wish, but a few, among whom Reynolds holds a distinguished place, have discussed both the practice and the theory of their art.

Now of these various groups, the philosophers neither painted pictures themselves, nor were renowned for exceptional taste and judgment with regard to them. The men of letters in some few instances did show practical good taste, but rarely or never, I think, in any but a narrow field. The evidence of the painters is more valuable, especially where a painter

* Walter Pater's enlightened and suggestive essay on "The School of Giorgione" is a remarkable exception, and deserves to be much better known than appears to be the case.

happens to be known, not only for his skill with the brush, but for his sound judgment upon the work of other men. In these two respects Reynolds stands pre-eminent, and his words have an authority such as few other writers can claim.

Ruskin, in a well-known passage, contrasts his theory with his pictures: "Nearly every word that Reynolds wrote was contrary to his own practice: he seems to have been born to teach all error by his precept, and all excellence by his example; he enforced with his lips generalisation and idealism, while with his pencil he was tracing the pattern of the dresses of the belles of the day; he exhorted his pupils to attend only to the invariable, while he himself was occupied in distinguishing every variation of womanly temper; and he denied the existence of 'the beautiful at the same instant that he arrested it as it passed and perpetuated it for ever."

There is some truth in the criticism, at least in so far as it relates to Reynolds's work outside portraiture. He is certainly seen at his worst whenever he attempts to realize the ideal beauty of which he talked; and though, with characteristic modesty, he ascribed this failure to his own want of capacity, he at least failed only where every one else had failed before him.

Let us consider the efforts made at one time or another to turn this notion of ideal beauty to practical account. All academies of art, from the late Renaissance to our own day, have cultivated it; one and all have failed to stand the test of time. The men who have achieved lasting fame are those who have broken away from academic precepts, not those who have followed them. In Italy the names of Tiepolo, Canaletto and Guardi, as in France those of Watteau and Chardin, have lived, while their learned contemporaries are forgotten.

If any parallel were needed to the case of Reynolds, who preserved by portraiture the fame he would have sacrificed as a follower of ideal beauty, the case of Ingres might be quoted. In Ingres, France possessed, by general consent, a draughtsman able to hold his own with the greatest, and one gifted too with abundant power and character. Yet time is gradually proving that the fame of Ingres is dependent upon his incisive individual portraits, and not upon his generalized ideal compositions—faultless, in a way, as these latter may be. Why is it too that our own gifted and generous Leighton touches us with an occasional portrait, like that of Sir Richard Burton, far more than by his most able efforts in the grand style? Why is it that Germany, whose painters for generation after generation have followed with logic, persistence, and often with considerable power, the road pointed out by æsthetic philosophers, has produced so infinitely little that has any æsthetic value?

The common fault found with all these attempts at

realizing an ideal beauty superior to that found in any member of the human race is insipidity. "Yet," the philosopher may answer, "insipidity is not found in Greek art, where by universal consent ideal beauty has been most completely mastered; it is the talent of the moderns, not their ideal, which is at fault."

However, even Reynolds saw that this ideal beauty in Greek art was not one, but many; that there were distinct types; that there might be an ideal Hercules and an ideal Gladiator, as well as an ideal Apollo. Had he followed up this train of thought to its logical conclusion, or had he known what we now know about the development of Hellenic sculpture, he might have made a discovery which would have solved his difficulties.

Like all the painters and critics of his day, Reynolds was misled by knowing the masterpieces of classical art only through the medium of Græco-Roman copies. Now that we can compare the Greek originals with the later versions that even half a century ago were supposed to represent them, we can easily see where the mistake started. In all, or nearly all, these Græco-Roman copies, even where the general proportions and the attitude correspond to the originals, we miss just those minute subtleties of surface and contour which make the difference between the great artist and the clever copyist—between art which is living and art which is dead. However capable the imitation, we always find not only a certain stiffness, coarseness or emptiness in the modelling, but a certain tendency to eclectic generalisation. Whatever the individual character of the Greek originals, the copies of them all seem to incline in some indefinable way towards a single type, so that, without some acquaintance with the iconography of the subject, it may be difficult at times to decide offhand whether a Græco-Roman imitation relates to the time of Pheidias or to that of Lysippos.

This eclectic sameness, this vague generalized resemblance between all the late versions of Hellenic sculpture, would have been enough in itself to suggest a wholly mistaken idea of the great Greek artists. When we remember that even these copies were not seen by Reynolds and his contemporaries in their pristine condition, but only after they had been repeatedly altered, polished, restored, and trimmed to suit the taste of successive generations of luxurious prelates and degenerate princes, like the antiques still existing in the older Roman museums, the wonder is, not so much that the principles deduced from them should have been incorrect and useless, as that they should have been accepted as a foundation for any æsthetic canon at all.

It is easy thus to understand how Reynolds and his brother inquirers derived from the eclectic sameness of Græco-Roman work the notion of a perfect ideal beauty;

just as from its trimming, polishing and restoration, most of them associated that ideal with surface finish and prettiness. Had they known Greek art as we know it now, how widely different would their conclusions have been! In the place of eclectic sameness they would have discovered infinite variety; in the place of one more or less uniform and generalized style, they would have discovered a number of emphatic and distinct personalities.

The great Greek sculptors, in short, like the great artists of all other periods, are great, not because they all conform to some single ideal canon, but because, supposing such a canon is conceivable, each departs from it by emphasising the particular qualities or beauties which appeal to him. It is by this personal emphasis, this individual character, that we distinguish the style of a Myron, a Paionios, a Pheidias, a Polycleitos, or a Praxiteles. Not until we come to the time when the successors of Alexander the Great founded museums and academies does this personal emphasis begin to disappear, and as it does so, the art concurrently declines in beauty.

That the general average of Hellenic sculpture is surpassingly high, and that in certain phases of it, as in the terracottas, we have to deal with schools rather than individuals, does not alter the main fact. The terracottas bear no nearer relation to the great Greek figure sculptures than the French school of the eighteenth century does to Watteau. In that school we find a high average of spirit, charm and dexterity; but its art is essentially a minor art, and so is that of the terracotta figurines. The great artist is great in virtue of the individuality of his achievement, as well as of its excellence. To resemble another artist or school of artists closely is a certain sign of inferiority; though, where the standard is so lofty as it was in classical Greece, such inferiority is finer than supremacy under a less fortunate star. In the same way the minor artists of the Italian quattrocento inherit a general tradition of sound design, sound workmanship and pleasant colouring, which makes even a hastily painted cassone front delightful to the eye, although the individuality behind it is feeble or non-existent.

We must then give up absolutely and for ever the application of a fixed canon of ideal beauty, either in the human form or in anything else, as a touchstone for the Fine Arts. The idea of such a perfect type may indeed exist in the mind, but only as a centre of departure for those variations from it by which each master of the future will reveal a new form of loveliness. Instead, therefore, of expecting new talent to conform exactly to some existing standard or ideal of beauty, we must recognise that genius must inevitably be accompanied by a difference from all previous standards; while close correspondence with any of these standards, however immediately pleasing it may appear, will be a certain proof of mediocrity.

The secondary effects of reliance upon a canon of perfect ideal beauty have been no less calamitous than its primary statement. It was soon recognized by thoughtful minds that this canon not only failed to account for the admitted excellences of many great works of art, but was actually inconsistent with them. To explain the discrepancy, " Truth to Nature," interpreted in a thousand different senses, was called in; and until the latter half of the nineteenth century (when " Truth to Nature" began to occupy the field alone), the efforts of painters and critics alike were devoted to reconciling somehow these shifting, intangible opposites.

The result has been utter chaos, disastrous to artists both directly and indirectly. Directly, because talent, when it does appear, is ushered into a world of controversy and confusion, where years which might have been devoted to active progress have to be wasted in searching for a sound road: indirectly, because this uncertainty breeds misconception, mistrust and hostility between the painters of different schools and different generations. If one half of the energy which artists have devoted during the last hundred years to abusing and discrediting their fellows had been spent upon creative work, how much richer would the world be now, and how much higher would the artist's reputation stand for moderation and good sense!

In the interests of peace, tolerance, and the general well-being of painters as a class, some reconsideration of the whole theory of the Fine Arts is imperatively needed. Two hundred years of ingenious juggling with indefinite, and perhaps indefinable, terms like Beauty and Truth have led us to disastrous anarchy. Until this old disorder of thought is utterly swept away out of mind, we can have no stable platform for the future structure, in which Classics and Romantics, Realists and Idealists, and all the myriad parties and factions by which artists are now divided, will finally and harmoniously unite.

Tradition is frequently appealed to as the one thing needful, and if the word be rightly understood, the appeal is reasonable enough. Tradition, however, far from being a panacea for all artistic ills, is strictly limited in its scope. In its essence tradition is no more than the body of principles which secure conformity between art and its contemporary environment. The architecture and the conditions of life in any given period control the scale, the material, the subject-matter and the treatment of the pictures and sculpture produced to suit them. As generation succeeds generation, the method of securing this conformity with local needs becomes embodied in definite formulæ, at first mere trade recipes, which amount in time to a technical tradition.

This tradition, like a canon of perfect beauty, is valuable only as a starting-point. The man who never goes beyond the tradition of his age can never be more than a sound craftsman. For Genius, tradition is always a base from which a further advance may be safely made. In primitive art these advances will enlarge the tradition; in mature art they may be its ruin. A Giotto or a Masaccio departs from the tradition of his contemporaries only to widen and strengthen it. A Michelangelo, a Raphael or a Titian advances so far that no succeeding explorers in the same field can hope to gain a new laurel; the soil is exhausted and the tradition doomed.

But a tradition may die in another way. The conditions of civilization which originally brought it into being may alter so much in course of time that a tradition, which was once in harmony with its environment, at last is so no longer. The tradition of historical and religious painting, for instance, survived in Europe for nearly two centuries after it had ceased to correspond to men's real thoughts and needs. Conversely, the revival of any past tradition, however splendid its record, is a perilous business; for unless it can be adapted to the decorative and intellectual needs of the period of its renaissance, it will be futile and pedantic. However much we may learn from the tradition of other ages, the tradition of our own age must correspond with our own thoughts, our own tastes, and our own material needs. Our tradition, in short, must be in some sense a new thing, or it can be no tradition at all.

The following chapters touch only one small section of the Fine Arts, that of painting as practised among us to-day, and touch even that in the most rudimentary fashion. Yet this restriction to a comparatively narrow and material province has one merit. It permits a more close scrutiny and a more definite testing of any new principles that may be tentatively advanced, than would be possible in a larger and more abstract study. The older theories have really fallen into disrepute and disuse because they consistently failed the working artist in his hour of need ; and, unless it can emerge successfully from the ordeal of the studio and the workshop, any newer theory will share the same fate.

The true logical foundation of the Fine Arts is inextricably connected with their concrete function, materials and processes; and no abstract philosophising which has neglected these essential factors, has produced any fruit but fine words, conflicting judgments and bad painting. It is upon the practical sciences of picture-making, of sculpture-making and the like, and not upon any group of abstract ideas, that the æsthetic philosopher of the future will have to erect the complete all-embracing theory which will enable artists to be peaceable, art patrons to be confident, and art-critics to be unanimous.

PART I

EMPHASIS OF DESIGN

Those who are enamoured of practice without science are like a pilot who goes into a ship without rudder or compass.

LEONARDO DA VINCI

A

CHAPTER I

THE VALUE OF EMOTION

THERE is a common foundation from which all the arts rise, and that is the need of self-expression on the part of the artist,—expression of his own personal experience, whether it be by words, as with literature; by sound, as with music; by pigment or plastic shape, as with the graphic arts. But there is a further condition attendant upon this expression of which we do not always take account, namely, that the artist's personal experience must be emphasised by strong feelings, by enthusiasm, by emotion, or the result is not art.

When experience is set forth without emotion we have in literature the prosaic, in art the photographic, and in music the academic. So far as poetry is concerned I do not think I need defend the theory at length; but its bearing upon painting is perhaps less clear. If we accept it for the moment it will give us some such description of painting as follows:

*Personal Experience Emphasised by Emotion
in Flat Decoration.*

For our present purpose the important word in that

3

description is the word "emotion": but, as its consideration may take a little time, it will be more convenient first to discuss briefly the other portions of this description, reserving "emotion" for fuller treatment afterwards.

In the first place let us take the word "experience." For the painter that implies two things ; first, knowledge of some part or aspect of the world we live in, and secondly, command of the processes by which that knowledge may be translated into paint. The great painter will possess both these forms of knowledge in a high degree. A Michelangelo, a Titian, or a Rembrandt, not only has profound insight into the recesses of the human mind, but lives in an age when a technical tradition exists which may be refined and enlarged till it becomes capable of presenting this insight perfectly.

Second-rate painters, on the other hand, lack one of these forms of experience. Sometimes, like many of the Italian eclectics, of the minor Dutchmen of the seventeenth century. or of the French Academic painters of the eighteenth and nineteenth, they are content, when once they have acquired enough technical skill to satisfy the public demand for sound handiwork, to let their brains go to sleep, and to continue producing empty pictures into which no touch of living interest or knowledge is allowed to enter.

On the other side we have rare independent minds

like our own Blake, whose imaginative experience is of the richest, but who by some defect of character or of training have not the means of expressing it perfectly and consistently. Of the two failings this latter of course is infinitely the more tolerable, and in quoting Blake it must be understood that I do not refer to such incomparable designs as the *Creation of Eve* in the Milton series, or *The Morning Stars* in the Job, but to the bulk of his work, where the execution is manifestly unequal to the conception. In these days, however, there are few who would not rather possess an average drawing by Blake than a good specimen of Albano or Bouguereau.

The *débris* of this second class, the art student who has quick fingers and no brains, and the amateur who has brains but will not stand the labour of regular practice, fade off gradually into the third class—the bad painters who are too stupid to think or too idle to draw, and who for all practical purposes may be classed with the children who scribble railway trains on slates; *non ragioniam di lor !*

This double experience, however, must be personal experience, and that is what hardly one artist in a thousand succeeds in retaining. The student has to learn the technical part of painting from some master or masters in some sort of a school, and few when learning the method of their seniors are strong enough to avoid learning to see like them also. The greater the master the more striking his example, and the more abject the submission of his followers.

School follows school and generation generation, all treading the same path of empty unthinking servility, until the tradition which, with the first master, was fresh and living becomes in later hands an anæmic shadow of its founder's practice. Then, perhaps, the man of independent mind is born. He sees the futility of the work around him, revolts against it, and starts a new tradition, doomed in its turn to follow the same stages of decay as its victim.

It was thus that Reynolds, Gainsborough, and Hogarth revolted against the dying school of Kneller and Hudson. Their tradition in time became moribund, and was overthrown finally by the Pre-Raphaelites. The Pre-Raphaelite influence in its turn is sick to death, and Impressionists, Orientalists, Decorators, and Revivalists (if I may use the term without disrespect of those who practise the older methods of using oil and tempera) fight over its death-bed for the succession.

The common feature of all these movements is that the great men are always the pioneers—the people with something of their own to say. The followers, who echo (perhaps with some minor differences) what the leaders have already said, are men of the second rank. Not only then must our experience cover both the matter and the manner of painting, but it must be personal,—must bear the impression of our own character, of our own feeling, of our own vision—or it will be second-rate as well as second-hand.

The difficulty of being personal, of learning the technical part of the art of painting from the example of another without at the same time assimilating, even unconsciously, that teacher's habit of thought, is one which active minds often feel. It is not uncommon, for example, to see an art student paint in the most garish and violent colours, not from any innate bad taste, nor always from the vulgar desire to attract attention, but simply from the wish to show his independence, to prove that he is not a slave to the manner in which he has been trained. Such eccentricities are perhaps preferable to slavish imitation of a teacher's style, but they are often productive of harm in another way. When an able student gives way to them, he may attract weaker spirits to follow in his steps. He will then not only injure their prospects, but may himself be misled by their imitation and their praise to regard his extravagance as a merit.

Then this personal experience must be summed up, epitomised, emphasised, in terms of decoration. This too we are in danger of forgetting nowadays. We are satisfied if our painting has an obvious resemblance to nature, without troubling ourselves (as we ought to do) whether we have made it a space of delightfully interwoven lines and tones and colours, perfectly adapted to the position it is destined to occupy, and to the surroundings among which it will be placed.

In the case of small portable works of art immediate surroundings need not be considered minutely. It is well that pictures in general should not be too dark, because in all civilised countries they will hang in houses where the light will be more or less subdued. Nor need the artist think too much of the furniture and wall-papers near which his work may be placed, since it will be separated from them by its frame. An easel picture, in a sense, is a focus of interest in the room where it hangs; therefore its general pitch of colour may without disadvantage be made as strong as the painter can safely manage. So long, too, as the colours are harmonious in themselves and are surrounded by a broad band of framing, they will adapt themselves wonderfully to almost any position or scheme of interior decoration.

From the decorative point of view then the picture and its frame make up a single unit: the one is not complete without the other. It is much to be regretted that this aspect of the painter's art does not receive in these days the attention which was bestowed upon it in the early Renaissance.

Then the large mural painting was nicely adapted to the architectural features round it, while the altar-piece and the portrait had frames specially designed, often at great cost, to display their charms to the best advantage. In the same way the black frames used by the Dutch Masters were used not only because they were exactly suited to the sober furnishing of a Dutch interior, but also because they are the best possible foil to the tones of red and brown and blue and gray of which the majority of Dutch pictures are composed.

The subject is one which it would be inappropriate to handle in detail in this place: but it is impossible to lay too much stress on the fact that a picture from the decorative point of view must always be regarded in connection with its frame. I firmly believe that a good deal of the dislike which the public have for modern painting is due to the abominable frames in which it is presented to them. The art of the furniture-maker, the upholsterer, and the paper-stainer, if often mechanical, has reached a high point of development; that of the frame-maker rarely rises above the ideals of the seaside lodging-house.

We now come to the phrase "emphasised by emotion," and in that phrase lies the essence of the whole matter. It was originally suggested to me by an article on the emotional base of poetry,* but it applies with equal force to painting. The great poet has experience of life, but wherein does he differ from the great philosopher, the great historian, or the man

* See *The Academy*, July 27, 1907. The author, Mr. A. Clutton Brock, afterwards discussed the relation of emotion to painting in *The Burlington Magazine* for October 1907 (vol. xii. pp. 23–26).

of science? They possess experience too, and may express it well, yet their work may be utterly lacking in poetry. If we test the matter by examining a few examples of fine poetry we shall find that fine poetry not only expresses the thoughts of the writer, but expresses them with a certain compelling power and emphasis. First we note a vivid conciseness of phrasing which concentrates the attention entirely upon the decisive words : then the beat of their rhythm or the sequence of the vowel sounds will accentuate their purport, by calling in the aid of music to rein-force the merely intellectual significance which words by themselves possess.

This consummate interweaving of words and music, this vehement concentration of thought in its most irresistible form, is the product of emotion, and the greatest achievements of all the great poets are replete with this emotional quality. When, as in our English Bible, we find passages of sublime emotion without regular rhythm we have poetical prose; and the poetical element in literature decreases *pari-passu* with the decrease of emotion, till we come to the plain state-ments made without any emotion at all, which we term prosaic. With them we may fitly compare the thoughts which are expressed in metrical form without emotion These are commonly called bad poetry, but are not really poetry at all.

Emotion then is the keystone of the art of poetry: it

is also the keystone of the art of painting. The former truth is more or less generally recognised. Only a dunce or a pedant would sit down in cold blood to write an epic. Yet thousands and thousands of painters seem to sit down in cold blood and expect to paint good pictures.

The one effort is no less ridiculous than the other. We may perhaps try in cold blood to make an accurate drawing, a careful study of some natural fact; we may even find that in such moods our fingers and wrists work steadily and accurately, but the result will always reflect the coldness of our hearts and, though we may view it with some poor pride in our own accomplishment, it will never kindle a shred of genuine enthusiasm either in ourselves or in any one else. When working without emotion we may represent things, but we cannot interpret them or inspire them with life. We set ourselves in fact to rivalling the camera, and enter upon that prosaic contest with a heavy handicap against us.

The true painter's emotion sums up and concentrates his experiences in terms of paint, as the poet sums up his experiences in terms of rhythm. It seizes on the facts of the subject that are essential to pictorial expression and rejects all others. It emphasises these selected facts by all the devices of the painter's art, by rhythm of line, by the spacing and the disposition of masses, by light and shade, by colour, and by the very handling of the paint, till the result is a harmonious

pictorial statement in which the various elements unite
to serve the artist's purpose.

The taste to choose only the essential things and
reject all others, to recognise by instinct what material
substances these essentials demand for their perfect
expression, the scale on which they must be treated,
their place on the picture surface, the arabesque of line
and light and shadow and colour which fits them,—
the taste to decide all these questions is part of an
artist's equipment. It is his professional outfit and, as we
shall see, it is largely a matter of rule and precept, which
may be acquired by study, just as a poet acquires by
study a vocabulary and the rules of grammar and metre.

But to make good pictures the painter needs the
stimulus of emotion just as does the poet. Only when
his thought is white hot can he succeed in effecting
that perfect fusion of visual idea and professional
experience which makes great painting. It is for this
reason and not for any decline in technical skill that
the art of an age which has been stirred by great events,
when men's minds are on fire with anticipation of
future triumphs or with recent memories of triumphs
achieved, always rises above that of periods of unbroken peace. In such easy times clever, pretty
and humorous work may be produced, but all great
work is stimulated by the excitement of conflict,
whether the conflict be one of nation with nation, or
merely of party with party.

The artist in short runs into the most acute peril the moment he has nothing to struggle against. That is the real trouble of those who practise art with success. The stimulus to do battle for their convictions is removed, and their work, which should be the outcome of a constant effort to conquer adverse circumstances, becomes an easy routine. The example of Millais is notorious, both because his original talent was so wonderful, and because, when tempted by wealth and popularity, he lost not only the creative energy which inspired his early designs, but even his mastery over his materials. His later works can be cheap in execution as well as in sentiment.

Only the very strongest men can resist this insidious failing. Reynolds never started a picture without a resolution to make it the best picture he had ever painted, and his principle is one that may safely be recommended. The artist who does not cultivate his emotions and keep them active must run to seed. No swiftness of hand, accuracy of eye, or technical experience can make amends for their loss.

Yet emotion by itself is as worthless to the would-be painter, as it is to the would-be violinist. Without technical experience and constant exercise his hand and eye will fail to express the idea he has in his mind. He must therefore be master of the rules and principles of his art before his emotion can turn that art to profit, and it is here that many find a difficulty.

The principles of design and colour, nay the mere mechanical accuracy of hand and eye necessary for correct drawing, can only be attained at the cost of persistent effort, and by a succession of exercises that may come to seem dull and tedious. The enthusiasm with which the young painter sets out vanishes in the stress of long study, and he may leave his art-school at last with a sound knowledge of technical process, but with no artistic emotion left to inspire his creations with life.

Those who feel that the technical part of their work is overwhelming them, might be wise to ask whether they would not have a better chance of preserving their personality and emotion by adopting some simple medium? The life and spirit which they fail to secure in oil painting, might be acquired and retained if they restricted themselves to black and red chalk, to etching, to pen and ink, or to silverpoint. The manipulation of these processes is easy compared with oil or water-colour, and so the artist can spare all his attention for the matter in hand. By limiting his method, he may enlarge his ambitions.

One other point remains to be mentioned. The current standard of good manners involves the repression of emotion in general, so that a writer suggesting that the artist should try to cultivate and enlarge his emotions might seem to advise rebellion against our accepted canons of good breeding. The painter's emotion, however, is a very different thing from the emotions of everyday life, from joy, sorrow, anger and the like. It concerns itself merely with the images that the artist forms in his mind's eye, and its cultivation implies only the intensifying and refining of those images. The artist, in fact, must not fear to give his admiration free scope, but must encourage himself to contemplate earnestly the noble forms, fine colour, marked character or subtle play of light and shade which he notices in nature. He must strive to keep his vision as fresh and emphatic as he can, knowing that if he does not feel things strongly himself, he cannot expect others to find strong feeling in his pictures.

When a painter has an adequate technical equipment, the mental images which he forms will insensibly be refined and made emphatic by the keenness of the feeling with which he treats them, and this process of refinement and emphasis will continue so long as the feeling lasts. Emotion and experience will control the rough design, the light and shade, the tones, the forms, the colours—the very handling of the brush being pressed into service, and adjusted to the task of adding still further accent and delicacy to the first rough conception.

Lastly we must never forget that the emotion which the painter has to cultivate is not the emotion of the poet, the musician, or the archæologist, but the emotion which is stirred by the pictorial aspect of things and by that aspect alone.

Whatever charm his subject may have for him by reason of its association with life or literature, he will make a bad picture of it if he allows the thought of this charm to come between him and the thought of its pictorial aspect. How many painters set out with a fine idea for a landscape and gradually destroy it by allowing the intrusion of details that are really irrelevant to its perfect pictorial presentation! How many subject-pieces are degraded to the level of common illustration from the wish to tell a story completely, the completeness entailing the introduction of figures or accessories that distort the original pictorial idea!

Pictorial quality is such an elusive thing that it is apt to vanish even when lines and masses are reproduced by a clever photographer. How infinitely greater is the peril in which it stands when the painter's thoughts stray in the direction of poetry, history, or science—when he forgets that his first business is simply and solely to make a beautiful picture, and that every addition which is not an addition to its external beauty is an excrescence. The danger naturally attacks most forcibly men who occupy themselves often with ideas which are not strictly pictorial, and it is for this reason perhaps that the painters who are fine orators or clever men of affairs are seldom able to keep their other accomplishments out of their pictures.

The friends of princes, like Raphael the scholar, Rubens the diplomatist, or Van Dyck the courtier, never move us quite so profoundly as those who, like Rembrandt, are masters of but one art, and have intensified their powers in solitude. If we realised the paramount necessity of such concentration and detachment we might perhaps more frequently try to secure them.

CHAPTER II

THE VALUE OF THEORY

SUPPOSING that some strong emotion such as that we have discussed impels us to express our thoughts and feelings in paint, how are we to set to work? How are we to provide those thoughts and feelings with just that artistic embodiment which most perfectly corresponds to them? Is this process of realisation something entirely apart from ordinary reasoning—something quite independent of deliberate intellectual effort, something which must come to us from outside by inspiration and is incapable of analysis or transmission to others? Or is there some science, tradition, or system of knowledge which will indicate the lines on which our mental images may be set in order and transmuted into good pictures?

The latter of these two alternatives is commonly the more unpopular. Yet even the numerous painters of to-day who congratulate themselves upon their freedom from the errors and the restraints of the tradition of the old masters, and who would be the first to repudiate the notion that theory can be of any practical help to an artist, are not quite true to their own flag. They imply the existence of at least some guiding principle or theory by the stock phrases which they use as touchstones both for their own work and for other people's. Such words as Truth, Nature, Values, Tone, Brushwork, *Plein-air*, Breadth, Finish, Decorative, Sincere, Direct, Strong, Luminous, are really but abbreviations for separate little codes of formulæ, rules, or devices for picture-making; and those who rely upon one or two of them exclusively, have rebelled against the idea of a complete science or tradition, only to become slaves to a fraction of such a science. The complete theory of painting will embrace impartially all these smaller and narrower theories, just as it will embrace artists so widely diverse as Rossetti and Courbet, Michelangelo and John Van Eyck.

The writer however who attempts to lay any definite and substantial foundation for the Fine Arts has always to face a certain prejudice. He seems to explain away, or to offer a mechanical substitute for those exceptional feats of the intellect which are commonly known as genius. Even the great Reynolds has not escaped this prejudice, although he foresaw and prophesied it. "To speak," he remarks, "of genius and taste, as in any way connected with reason and common sense, would be in the opinion of some towering talkers, to speak like a man who possessed neither." So Reynolds's own works, though they are almost

unequalled in point of inventive design and colour,
are still sometimes termed cold and devoid of feeling
simply because he had the courage to proclaim boldly
that a large portion of the field of art was under the
dominion of rules, and, to encourage beginners,
pronounced that nothing was denied to well-directed
labour. It is for these stimulating exaggerations, as
well as for their astonishing sanity and practical good
sense, that Reynolds's " Discourses " will ever be the
enthusiastic student's favourite book.

The phrase quoted from Sir Joshua's Second
Discourse was explained and modified by him four
years later in the Sixth Discourse.

" What we now call Genius begins, not where rules
abstractedly take end, but where known, vulgar and
trite rules have no longer any place. It must of
necessity be, that even works of Genius, like every
other effect, as they must have their cause, must
likewise have their rules ; it cannot be by chance that
excellencies are produced with any constancy or any
certainty, for this is not the nature of chance ; but the
rules by which men of extraordinary parts, and such
as are called men of Genius, work, are either such as
they discover by their own peculiar observations, or
of such a nice texture as not easily to admit being
expressed in words ; especially as artists are not very
frequently skilful in that mode of communicating ideas.
Unsubstantial, however, as these rules may seem, and

difficult as it may be to convey them in writing, they
are still seen and felt in the mind of the artist ; and he
works from them with as much certainty, as if they
were embodied, as I may say, upon paper. It is true,
these refined principles cannot be always made pal-
pable, like the gross rules of art ; yet it does not
follow, but that the mind may be put in such a train,
that it shall perceive by a kind of scientific sense, that
propriety which words, particularly words of un-
practised writers, such as we are, can but very feebly
suggest."

The argument is unanswerable. As the ages go on
we may be able to formulate sound principles of
picture-making and picture criticism, far in advance of
and far more subtle than any principles we can deduce
to-day, but each advance will not imply a nearer
approach to the secret of Genius. It will merely
provide talent with a further stepping-stone from
which to leap forward.

It cannot be too definitely stated at the outset that
a knowledge of principles is no substitute for invention. Principles by themselves cannot create a work
of art. They can only modify and perfect the vague
pictorial conceptions formed in the artist's mind, which
are the foundation upon which he builds. When these
first vague conceptions are once formed, and sketched
out in tentative shape, the service of theory begins.
By its help the first rough, incomplete idea is gradually

trained, corrected, and perfected, till it is transformed into a final and complete design. The general plan is adjusted and spaced, contours are made significant, the colour-scheme is thought out, and the material required is selected, so as best to enhance the particular end in view.

To the beginner, this process of selection and arrangement may seem pedantic and mechanical, and at first the traces of deliberate planning will almost certainly be evident in his work. Yet after a little while the brain will become used to the regular exercise which the application of formal tests entails, and will not only be strengthened by the exercise, but will learn to do quickly and instinctively what at first was only done by laborious, deliberate effort.

In a well-known passage, Leonardo points out how, by constant practice, the eye may be trained to measure spaces accurately. It is not then illogical to assume that the eye may be trained by similar practice, to recognise those harmonies of rhythm and relations of mass which make design decorative. To the gifted few this sense is given by nature, just as to a few is given the faculty of drawing correctly with but little effort or training, yet there is no doubt that most men with any feeling for art, however modest their natural gifts, could increase their power of recognising harmonious spacing by proper cultivation. The first attempts might be tedious, but speed would come with practice, and they would in the end seem to plan their compositions by native talent rather than any conscious process or system.

And if we make this admission how much does it not imply? Design is the first element, the ground-work, the foundation of all art, and if proficiency, not to speak of supreme excellence, can be attained in it by methodical practice, are we to despise any formal gymnastics that lead to so desirable an end? Let any one with a love of fine design visit an ordinary modern exhibition such as that of the Royal Academy, and judge for himself how many of the exhibitors can be termed even tolerably competent designers. The vast mass of the work exhibited is in one way or another accomplished, but how little of it shows even a trace of the noble spacing of lines and masses which we find everywhere in the National Gallery?

There has been undeniably a certain danger in the study of rules and principles. Those who have studied them much have frequently come to regard them as an end in themselves and not as a means to an end. This mistake has been due to more than one cause. Sometimes, as in the case of Paolo Uccello, enthusiasm for a particular principle may run riot at the expense of all others. Sometimes, as in the case of many eclectic painters, rules come to be regarded as a substitute for invention, and a few principles of composition may be employed upon a limited range of stock subjects, till the artist becomes a hack, possessing, it may be, considerable facility of hand but nothing else.

These perils have been incurred not by setting an excessive value on principles and theories of design, but by utterly misunderstanding their character or purpose. As we shall see these principles are *not* in the nature of moulds or patterns to which the subject matter of a picture has somehow to be adapted, and into which it has ultimately to be squeezed. Even Burnet's "Treatise on Painting," the most complete compendium in English of the traditional practices of the old masters, has its reasoning stultified, and its usefulness much diminished by this disastrous fallacy. The principles of design, instead of being fixed and rigid like geometrical figures, are infinitely flexible, *and always dependent upon the subject-matter of a picture*, being indeed no more than the means of emphasising that subject-matter perfectly. Having said this much to correct a general misconception as to the nature of theory we must turn to some other elementary factors in the making of a good picture.

CHAPTER III

INVENTION AND NATURE

Of all the elements which go to make an artist the faculty of invention is perhaps that most dependent upon innate natural gifts. Nevertheless it may be doubted whether any man who has a mind of average capacity and a genuine enthusiasm for art is wholly devoid of it. In certain great artists, as in Rubens for example, the inventive faculty is strongly developed; such men are capable of pouring out an infinite number and variety of designs. In others, as with Velasquez, it operates within narrower bounds. Sometimes, as with Blake, it makes too heavy a demand on the means of artistic expression: at others, as with the minor Dutchmen and many modern painters, it is dormant and subordinated to dexterity in representation.

That the inventive faculty can be stimulated artificially has been held by more than one great artist. Leonardo mentions the study of the markings produced by time and damp upon old walls; Reynolds, the study of the inventions of other artists; Gainsborough is said to have played with toy landscapes, with bits of stone for rocks or hills, and pieces of looking-glass for water; Alexander Cozens recommended the working up of chance blots artificially produced. The reading of history and poetry is another well-known recipe. Most of us as we read conjure up in our minds some image, usually vague and dim, of the scenes described in print. Could we but fix and materialise these conceptions on paper or canvas we should have taken the first step on the road to creative design.

Better, however, than books or pictures, discoloured walls or artificial devices of any kind, is the study of nature. It is from nature that we derive the pictorial symbols by which we must express our ideas in paint; nature too, especially at twilight when all petty details are obscured, is infinitely suggestive, and her suggestions have the vitality which a picture also must have if it is to retain its hold continuously upon the minds of men. The impressions we get from nature are at once more complete and more vivid than those we get from artificial sources, and, as a rule, are less troublesome to record.

Yet if we work entirely from nature we have to face a difficulty of another kind. When technicalities are once fairly mastered the actual process of painting from nature becomes almost mechanical and, if we paint with a model always before us, we are apt to get into the

habit of copying indiscriminately all that we see, without
troubling to stop and think whether what we are recording is really pictorial—is really improving our
picture.   In fact the moment that we cease thinking, we
forget to omit what ought to be omitted, and to select
just what ought to be selected to make a good picture,
and are placing ourselves on a level with a photographic camera.   Nor does the trouble end here.   When
a man has once yielded to this fatal habit it grows
upon him till he ceases to think at all, and goes on to
the end of his life painting more or less accurate tran-
scripts of nature, possessing it may be, some skill, but
no vitality or character.   He becomes one of the great
host of mediocre modern painters, who have to console
themselves with the thought that they are sincere,
conscientious and truthful when others find them
tedious.

Nevertheless if we look at nature too little we are
thrown on our own resources ;   we imitate ourselves
and become empty and mannered, as all schools and all
artists have done who did not constantly refresh their
minds in the presence of nature.   How then are we to
pick our way between the two extremes ?

I think we shall be wise if we adopt the system
upon which all great creative artists have worked, that
is to say to paint our pictures, not from nature herself,
but from memory, assisted by studies made in the
presence of nature.

Our studies from nature will fall under two distinct headings.

1. Notes of happy combinations of figures or masses, or light and shadow that we may chance to see, and that suggest possibilities of pictorial treatment.

These being for the most part only first aids to the memory will rarely require a high degree of finish. A few suggestive lines or blots of colour will be enough to serve as a reminder, while the fleeting character of many of the most attractive natural effects will, in itself, often compel a certain degree of swiftness in the work if the critical moment is to be recorded at all.

2. Sketches of details, which may, nay must be more complete. Since the degree of realisation needed for any single part of a picture cannot be settled finally till the picture is well on its way to completion, the artist runs less risk if his preliminary studies have been full and precise.

A hasty study however good of its kind may omit just the very things that happen to be needed in the particular picture for which the study was made. A careful study may contain much that afterwards may prove unnecessary, but the painter who has such a study can take what he pleases and leave the rest. He is at any rate on the safe side.

In thinking of a composition it is essential to fix the attention on the general disposition of the lines and masses, of the shadows and colours. This general disposition can be best emphasised in a rapid sketch. In an elaborate study it is apt to be confused by details which, when a picture comes to be painted, prove to be irrelevant and disturbing. The mere fact of working from a slight sketch keeps the mind on the *qui vive* and the memory active, while the absence of nature leaves the intellect free to select just those elements and no others which have pictorial significance. Of details, however, we cannot have too accurate a recollection. However much we decide in the end to conventionalise or simplify them, a knowledge of their essential character will survive in the abbreviated symbol we invent for them, and our work will suggest nature even where it does not attempt to imitate her.

The practice of all the great masters up to the middle of the nineteenth century bears out this contention. Almost without exception we find their studies of detail from nature to be exact and careful: their studies for compositions where they exist at all are slight and sketchy. In the former case their attention is concentrated upon recording particular facts: in the latter upon recording a general effect.

This practice we have almost given up—to our immense detriment. We try to make a single elaborate sketch serve the double purpose of recording particular facts as well as a general effect. The facts we may secure, or at least so many of them as are moderately permanent in character, but the general effect is, or ought to be, a thing of the moment, and is gone while we mix our colours.

If on the other hand we make a sketch, no matter how rough and hasty, of the general effect of a scene, we are at any rate sure of its general disposition, of its essential features, and of the spirit of the moment that made it seem desirable to us. We can then at our leisure make separate notes of such facts and details as we cannot trust our memory to retain. When we come to paint our picture we shall have the rough sketch to inspire us, and the finished studies to help us where our memory fails. Executed with these aids our work should lack neither spirit nor solidity, and we can comfort ourselves with the thought that we are working on the system which makes the best possible use of such brains as we possess.

CHAPTER IV

PICTORIAL CONDITIONS AND PICTORIAL EMPHASIS

HAVING come thus far we must ask ourselves under what conditions are we to use the suggestions of our imagination or of nature, in order to transmute them into good pictures? What principles in fact are to govern the selection and arrangement of our materials? That selection and arrangement are necessary, must be taken for granted. Nature is a vast inexhaustible storehouse, but to suppose that if she be taken as she is, the result will be a picture, is like supposing that a department of Whiteley's if bought *en bloc* will make a furnished house.

This cardinal fact has been recognised by every artist who has done fine work, yet it is so constantly neglected not only by students but by painters and critics who ought to know better, that it cannot possibly be emphasised too strongly. Nor has the case ever been put more neatly than by Whistler in his "Ten o'Clock," a masterly piece of criticism which would perhaps have received more attention from the world had it only been rather less witty.   The passage is well known to all admirers of Whistler's art but is so apposite to our purpose that it may perhaps be quoted.

"Nature contains the elements, in colour and form, of all pictures, as the keyboard contains the notes of all music.

"But the artist is born to pick, and choose, and group with science, these elements, that the result may be beautiful,—as the musician gathers his notes, and forms his chords, until he brings forth from chaos glorious harmony.

"To say to the painter that nature is to be taken as she is, is to say to the player that he may sit on the piano."

Now there are four qualities which all fine pictures in some degree possess, of which mediocre pictures lack at least one, and of which bad pictures lack at least three.   These may be taken as essential conditions of good work for ourselves, and as touchstones of a simple kind for testing the work of others.   The four qualities are—

(1) Unity ; (2) Vitality ; (3) Infinity; (4) Repose.

The order of their relative importance will vary with the function of each painting, the taste of each age, and the temper of each individual painter.   The age of Poussin would have given Unity the first place ; most landscape painters and the continental artists of to-day would certainly vote for Vitality; Leonardo, Michelangelo and Rembrandt aimed first at what we have termed Infinity; while almost all hieratic art must gain its end by the expression of Repose. With all mural painting too this last quality must be a primary consideration.

1. That Unity is a condition of all good painting is self-evident. Although a picture may have to form part of a scheme of decoration, and therefore bear a definite relation to other pictures or other portions of the scheme, it must also be complete in itself, a panel with a single decorative pattern, and a single purpose. However many figures, incidents, colours, or groups it may contain, these diverse elements must all be knit into a rhythmic, coherent whole. If two groups or masses divide the spectator's interest the result is confusing, and so falls short of complete success ; if more than two elements compete for mastery the confusion in the spectator's mind is still worse confounded. If in looking at a picture we are long in doubt as to which is the central motive, if a number of lights or shadows or colours press themselves upon our eyes with an equal degree of insistence, we may be sure that the work is lacking in unity and, whatever its other merits, has one very serious defect. Men of prolific imagination like Tintoret are more prone to suffer from lack of unity, than those who like Velasquez seem to work with cool deliberate science.

2. It was not without reason that the Chinese critic of the sixth century placed rhythmic vitality first in

his famous six canons of painting, for Vitality, the sense of life in a picture, is almost as important, nay perhaps even more important than unity. If the sense of life be absent the most able composition leaves us cold ; if it be present we can condone many other faults. Rubens in the Netherlands, Michelangelo in Italy will serve as types of artists possessing this quality in full measure, while among English landscape painters, Constable would serve as a characteristic example, and might be contrasted with Whistler, to whose otherwise perfect artistic equipment vitality was often in some degree lacking.

3. The third condition of painting, Infinity, is less easily defined. It implies an escape from too bald and precise statement ; a sacrifice, perhaps, of immediate force of effect to depth of impression : the introduction of an element of uncertainty or evanescence in spacing in tone, in colour or in line. It is the quality towards which delicacy of eye and hand contribute most, whether it be manifested in tremulous gradations of colour as with Titian and Watteau, of tone and line as with Leonardo, of shadow as with Rembrandt, or of atmosphere as with Turner. Of all pictorial qualities infinity is perhaps the rarest in these days, yet no art that has lacked it has retained the highest rank, and for want of it even a Sargent may have to be content with a place among brilliant painters, and not among the supreme artists.

4. Repose on the other hand is a quality which all painters of reasonably good taste can compass. It is a condition which, like unity, bears largely on the decorative value of a painting ; which insists that a picture shall be a portion of the wall on which it hangs, and shall not attempt to deny its function, by simulated projection of masses, by unpleasant turbulence of line, or by noisy importunate colour. If unity then may be said to give a painting coherent structure, vitality to inspire it with the breath of life, infinity to redeem it from shallowness, repose may be said to endow it with good manners.

Design is often spoken of as if it were something distinct and separate in itself, in the nature of a general pattern or a scale of patterns into which the subject-matter of a picture had somehow to be fitted. Many painters of to-day seem to hold this view, or something like it, for nothing is commoner than to see the new wine of modern portraiture and landscape put into the old bottles of Velasquez or Whistler or any other master who happens to be the fashion.

As we have seen design is not rigid but flexible ; not independent but absolutely dependent upon the subject-matter to which it is applied and the function it is called upon to serve. In its essence it is no more than the perfect emphasising of that subject-matter under the pictorial conditions previously discussed

It is by design that the realist makes his reality tell best; it is by design that the man of imagination makes his mental creations take complete pictorial shape; it is by design that the illustrator presents his story best, accentuating just the points that deserve accent and no others.

Pictorial design then may be described as *emphasis subject to pictorial conditions*. As such it will vary with each new theme to which it is applied, and will be co-extensive with the infinity of materials available for pictorial purposes. To deal with such a vast subject all at once is clearly impossible and we can only hope to understand something of it by separating the various parts of painting, and seeing how emphasis may best be obtained from each of them in turn. For practical purposes we may regard those parts as seven in number, so that the study of design may be resolved into seven separate studies, namely—

(i) Emphasis of Symbol: *i.e.*, by means of the devices or signs employed by the artist to convey his meaning, or to transmute natural phenomena into terms of art.

(ii) Emphasis of Plan: *i.e.*, by means of the surface disposition of the hues and masses in a picture.

(iii) Emphasis of Spacing: *i.e.*, by means of the proportion the masses bear to one another.

(iv) Emphasis of Recession : *i.e.*, by the apparent nearness or remoteness of the objects contained in a picture.

(v) Emphasis of Shadow.

(vi) Emphasis of Colour.

(vii) Emphasis of Material.

The emphasis in each of these cases will be subject to the pictorial conditions of Unity, Infinity, Vitality, and Repose. The various parts of our inquiry may therefore for clearness' sake be set out in tabular form as follows—

	I. UNITY.	II. VITALITY.	III. INFINITY.	IV. REPOSE.
Symbol	Unity of Symbol.	Vitality of Symbol.	Infinity of Symbol.	Repose of Symbol.
Plan	Unity of Plan.	Vitality of Plan.	Infinity of Plan.	Repose of Plan.
Spacing	Unity of Spacing.	Vitality of Spacing.	Infinity of Spacing.	Repose of Spacing.
Recession	Unity of Recession.	Vitality of Recession.	Infinity of Recession.	Repose of Recession.
Shadow	Unity of Shadow.	Vitality of Shadow.	Infinity of Shadow.	Repose of Shadow.
Colour	Unity of Colour.	Vitality of Colour.	Infinity of Colour.	Repose of Colour.
Material	Unity of Material.	Vitality of Material.	Infinity of Material.	Repose of Material.

A tabular analysis of this kind may not at first sight seem a particularly hopeful method of approach-

ing our subject, even to those who admit that an
orderly habit of thought may be no disadvantage to a
painter or critic. Nor can the classification adopted
here make any pretence to logical perfection. It is a
mere rough and ready makeshift frame-work, which
the reader will be able to amend and complete for
himself.

Some such formal analysis, however, is necessary
if we are to think clearly about a subject so infinitely
complex as pictorial design. We must have some
definite starting-point for diagnosis, some systematic
method of inquiry, if we are to localise faults, if we
are to understand the causes of those faults, and so to
discover the appropriate remedies. The working
artist will find the arrangement much simpler in
practice than it looks at first sight. With one important exception it has been utilised throughout the
following chapters. The variety of painter's materials
and processes is so great that the whole subject
could not be treated at once. Each method and process is therefore discussed by itself.

The two kinds of rhythm described on p. 66 might more properly
have been discussed in this chapter. The major rhythm in alliance
with the principle of unity controls the decorative character, the
pattern of a painting, just as the minor rhythms in alliance with
vitality determine its quality. If the major rhythm be absent we
have an illustration, not a picture. See pp. 317, 318.

CHAPTER V

EMPHASIS OF SYMBOL

THE question of the pictorial symbols which the painter employs is not always rightly understood. Critics often speak as if some absolute correspondence might exist between the things which a painter sees in nature and the representation which he makes of them. In some cases, indeed, this absolute correspondence may exist, as when we see some *trompe l'œil* in the shape of a piece of still life, a portrait, or the landscape in a panorama so realistically treated as, under certain conditions of place and lighting, to be indistinguishable from nature.

Yet this kind of literal facsimile is neither judged by the common consent of educated men to occupy a high place among existing forms of art, nor is it possible to obtain it with most subjects and under most circumstances. We may force our tones as much as we please, but we cannot attain to the pitch either of nature's sunlight or of her deep shadows, while with many mediums, such as etching, there can from first to last be no question at all of actual imitation

The painter is thus compelled willy-nilly to suggest nature by his art rather than to imitate her, and the symbols by which he makes the suggestion cannot have any absolute correspondence with nature, but only a correspondence that is subject to limitations of material and of the purpose in view.

Yet some correspondence must exist between a pictorial symbol and the object it represents, or the symbol would fail to convey to the observer the impression of the object. That the correspondence, too, is rather a close one may be inferred from the uniform advice of all the great artists who have left a record of their opinions, " Go to nature," and from the fact that " Truth to nature " has been the motto of almost all teachers of art in all periods.

Yet even if we recognise the limitations of materials, and admit that " Truth to nature " must be subject to them, as it is even in a photograph, the phrase does not solve our difficulties. There have been many painters who have succeeded in imitating nature as closely as their materials permitted, but hardly any of them have a place among the world's great masters. Every year there are hundreds and hundreds of pictures exhibited in London exhibitions which are more true to the aspect of our every-day world than is Titian's *Bacchus and Ariadne.* But we know that their painters are not greater artists than Titian any more than a good photograph of such a place as that glorified by Rembrandt in his *Three Trees* would be superior to his etching. "Truth to nature," in fact, is a phrase which cannot be pushed to an extreme in matters of art. "The business of a great painter," as Reynolds points out, "is to produce a great picture, and he must not allow himself to be cajoled by specious arguments out of his materials."

Works of art are subject to conditions of function and material which cannot be disregarded. The form of a flower may suggest to the goldsmith a shape for a noble cup, but to imitate the flower in metal would be to make a cup from which no one could drink in comfort. So with a picture or a drawing. Nature may suggest a design, but the materials, and the purpose which the picture or drawing has to serve, set limits to actual imitation of nature. These cannot be exceeded without breaking the harmony which ought to exist between matter and manner, between the subject and its perfect pictorial expression. The pictorial symbols by which we express nature will thus have a relation both to nature and to art. If we neglect the relation to nature our work will be shallow, mannered, or absurd ; if we neglect the relation to art it will be bad painting.

I

That pictorial symbols must have unity, must be of the same kind throughout any single work of art, should be self-evident. Yet the incongruity of introducing two different forms of symbol into the same picture is not always recognised.

We do not, perhaps, think a drawing by Gainsborough or Rembrandt would be improved if we were to substitute trees cut out from photographs for their eloquent shorthand, but we do sometimes see pictures in which jewellery is represented by real stones set in the paint. Tricks like this are really as barbarous as the landscapes made out of sea-weed which amused our great grandmothers, and deserve the same respect.

A more subtle, if less serious form of error creeps in when one part of a picture is a careful imitation of nature while another is pure convention. The unreality of French *genre* painting of the eighteenth century of the school of Watteau is accentuated by the difference between the careful painting of the figures and the conventional handling of the landscape. In the work of Gainsborough this sense of artificiality is lessened, because both figures and landscape are treated with a similar loose suggestive touch which serves as a bond between them.

The same incongruity is frequently seen in pure landscape, in the work of many English artists of the middle part of the nineteenth century, who combine a natural sky and distance with conventional trees and a conventional foreground. Copley Fielding will serve as an example. Greater men like Turner and Crome use conventions, but they use them so consistently that the whole is all of a piece, and we are not conscious of any discrepancy.   The examples of Blake, of Daumier, and of Puvis de Chavannes might also be quoted to show how the character and treatment of figures must be reflected in their landscape setting.   Indeed not the least difficulty of imaginative art is to secure this identity of symbolism where there is great diversity of generic character: to render for instance a cloud, a rivulet or a tree in precisely the same abstract terms that may be required for the human figure.

If for purposes of design we have to employ fantastic or conventional symbols it may thus be unwise to attempt to imitate nature too closely when we come to colour them.   The toppling crags and twisted trees on a piece of Chinese porcelain would look ridiculous if any attempt were made to colour them with the hues of nature; coloured as they are with the most dazzling and impossible colours they may be superb works of art.   Conversely if the symbol be drawn from nature with extreme verisimilitude it must be coloured, if at all, with something like the same accuracy.   The drawings of Cotman often look hot or garish, just because the details are so accurately drawn from nature that we expect a corresponding likeness to nature's colour. Sometimes this artificial colouring is made to look almost natural by contrast with a foreground group, coloured with quite impossible violence, but the device, for obvious reasons, is not a safe one, though it has Turner's example also to sanction it. Directly the contours cease to be precise, as in Cotman's late work (and still more in that of Turner), the colouring may be almost as independent of nature as the artist pleases without this loss of congruity. Wilson's mannerisms in painting trees would not annoy us so much were his pictures less true to nature in their rendering of atmospheric tone and colour.

To artists this question often presents problems of no little difficulty. In painting interiors with figures the background, if painted as precisely as the figures, will tend to overwhelm them, yet if conventionalised it will look weak and artificial unless the figure is painted with a similar convention, as was done by Reynolds and Gainsborough. To hold the balance evenly needs no little judgment, and few besides John Van Eyck, two or three Dutch masters and Chardin have done it with complete success. The same problem is ever present in portraiture, though there it can be evaded more easily by placing the sitter in front of a plain wall or a curtain.

II

A pictorial symbol must also have vitality. If it is to represent a man it must convey the impression of a living man, and not of a dummy ; if it is to represent a tree it must at all costs preserve the impression of organic structure, of some thing alive and in its degree sentient. The artist must realise, as the modern man of science has done, that vitality in one sense or another pervades all nature, otherwise his rendering of nature will be inert or dead. He must recognise the life not only of animal and vegetable forms, but of stones and water, of mountains and clouds.

The slightest scrawl that conveys this sense of vitality is a thing of interest; the most elaborate painting that fails to convey it is dull. Not without reason did the Chinese place this quality foremost among their canons of art, and their painters have proved that almost every other attribute of an object may be sacrificed yet, so long as vitality be retained the pictorial representation will be successful.

Let us first consider how this bears upon the art of portraiture, and ask ourselves how in a portrait the character of vitality is best attained. A moment's thought will show that a rapid sketch in pen and ink or some such emphatic medium, will suggest more vitality, more of the sitter's force and character than anything except a powerful finished picture. A chalk drawing worked up with the stump until it renders the texture of the sitter's flesh, or a highly-finished water-colour sketch which would imitate the colour of the sitter's dress and complexion, will be far less vivid and lively.

If we think out the reasons of this superiority we shall find them to be somewhat as follows.

1. The pen lines seize only on the essential features

2. They state them with the utmost possible clearness.

3. The very swiftness of the strokes conveys to the spectator an impression of vigour analogous to that exerted by the draughtsman.

A pen and ink sketch by an untrained hand if it catches the essential points of a man's features, and states them decidedly, may thus possess vitality, while an unskilful photograph in which every plane and contour of the face is rendered with perfect accuracy may be dull and dead. Instead of stating only the essential points the photograph will record the un-essential also; it will be weak in tone compared with a picture and, however good in other respects, it will certainly fail to convey the sensation of vigour that is suggested by forcible handling.

The principle that applies to portraiture will apply also to figure and to landscape; and here we begin to see why it is that the bulk of the painting in our modern exhibitions, in spite of the skill, effort, and labour spent upon it, is so deplorably monotonous.

Misled by such ambiguous phrases as " sincerity " and "truth " the painter apes the camera. Instead of con-centrating himself on the essential features of his design, he wanders off in search of unessential detail; instead of stating these essentials forcibly, he buries them under a mass of trifles; instead of stating them swiftly and fluently he works them up laboriously to a conventional polish.

Yet it may be thought that such a creed as this implies a denial of nature. The truth is the exact contrary. Let us imagine the conditions previously mentioned one by one.

In the first place the artist has to seize only the essential features of the thing he paints. Yet how is he to recognise them unless he knows his subject-matter by heart, and sees its relation to the particular form of work he has in hand? Is not this knowledge, this faculty of wise selection, a greater faculty than that of undiscriminating imitation however exact? There can be no doubt whatever that it is so. Imitation of some sort can be compassed by any trained student; the judgment which can instinctively separate the pictorial from the non-pictorial is the attribute of a master.

Take, for example, such a thing as a rock. Fifty per cent. at least of the pupils in any good art school could, if they were set to the task, make a map of its cracks and stains and lichens and projections not much inferior in accuracy to a photograph. A great artist however, will take only just so much of its specific character or accidental peculiarity as suits the purpose he may have in hand. For an elaborate oil painting he may require to render it with some approach to completeness, but he will be on the look out to see where his materials will help him to make his rendering look easy and natural, to suggest texture and character by the very surface and quality of his pigment ; and to see that the brush strokes with which he draws its form are related not only to that form, but also to the scheme of the picture which they help to compose.

Working in such a medium as silverpoint, he will at once recognise that the texture and surface which can be so readily suggested in liquid pigment cannot be readily suggested by a metal point. He will therefore waste no time over them but, since the silverpoint naturally produces delicate lines, will pick out the delicate lines in his subject, and concentrate his powers upon them.

The treatment of the human figure must be governed by exactly the same principles. When silverpoint is used it must be used so that its particular charm of line is preserved. It will thus emphasise delicate contours, but will suggest modelling only by a few open strokes, like those which we find in the silverpoints of Leonardo and Raphael. To aim at complicated effects of tone, as some moderns have done, is to misuse the medium in the way etching has been misused by some contemporary etchers.

Where effects of tone are required they must be obtained by mediums which naturally suggest tone. Hence the great masters when rendering the subtle surfaces of the human body draw in chalk or wash, while to emphasise the insertion of muscles or tendons, or to mark bony structure, they use the more emphatic stroke of the quill or reed pen. When painting, colour, surface and structure can all be rendered ; but in using a less complete medium the artist has constantly to be selecting only those attributes of the human form which suit the medium and no others. So far indeed is this process of selection carried by the best draughtsmen, that they will not try to draw one inch more of the model than the piece or feature that interests them. If they are studying the back, they will draw the back alone and leave the head, hands and feet unfinished.

The still prevalent custom of setting students to make large finished drawings of the whole figure is bad, just because it gives no play to this faculty of selection. The draughtsman instead of concentrating his interest on the passages which interest him, has to labour at representing many things that interest him little or not at all : the loss of emphasis so occasioned reacts upon the spectator, and the drawing proves a dull thing however capably done. The great masters themselves, sometimes, are not free from this failing. Even Michelangelo and Raphael have left us highly finished studies which exhibit their skill rather than their genius. A study which says too much may seem perhaps more easy to work from than one which says too little. But the loss of spirit that inevitably accompanies loss of emphasis, may in the end prove a heavier handicap for the practised artist, if not for the student too, than paucity of detail.

Thus for the true artist every medium dictates its own essentials, has its own set of pictorial symbols, and these cannot be transferred to the service of any other medium without risk of disaster. A broad oil sketch of a rock, such as we have mentioned, would not be very helpful material from which to work up a good silverpoint drawing, or *vice versâ*. Our sketches and studies therefore should always have a distinct relation to the medium in which they are to be worked out, as well as to our memories.

As to essentials then, we may briefly say that all work with the point will naturally seize upon contour and structure, as the things most readily suggested by lines; while in working with broad layers of tone the proportion, value and quality of the masses will be the things first sought for. Texture is a thing essential only in a limited class of subjects and, even there, should never be sought for till the greater essentials have been firmly secured. All painting which in any degree relies for its attractiveness upon imitation of texture is inconsiderable; yet, since texture is a thing which the veriest ignoramus can recognise when imitated in paint, the pictures which make it prominent are usually sure to be praised by the multitude for the moment.

So in drawing a head or a hand, the artist will try to mark first of all the structure and contour, and will not devote his energies to expressing the smoothness of the skin or matching its tone. In painting the same subject however, tone becomes an essential and texture may become so too. There is no fixed rule as to essentials. They vary infinitely with the subject and the materials, and all great painting is a constant process of discovery and invention: discovery of the essentials of the matter in hand, and invention of the pictorial symbols best adapted to represent them in the chosen medium.

A tree, for instance, is something too minutely detailed for exact imitation; it has to be represented by a symbol. Now if we compare for a moment the symbols used to represent trees by three or four famous landscape painters, we shall see how large a choice is left to the artist in search of essentials. For Hobbema the essentials of foliage are intricacy combined with serration of woody growth in the boughs; hence the minute involutions of touch by which he realises those essentials. For Gainsborough grace of mass, a delicacy of substance that responds to the gentlest breath of wind, and the capacity of leaves to retain and reflect the light which permeates through their interstices, are the essentials. His foliage symbol is thus elegant in form; in character luminous and airy.

With De Wint a tree tells as a heavy mass of cool green, and his usual symbol for trees disdains alike the intricacy of Hobbema and Gainsborough's lightsome grace. Constable's symbol is more complete

His trees have freshness, mass, motion, and not in-
frequently grace, intricacy and individuality; but the
blending of all those qualities makes them often somewhat unmanageable as decorative units. Constable's
contemporaries and successors either contented themselves with a less comprehensive formula, as did
Turner and the Impressionists, or. have produced
·second-rate pictures.

We must in fact not only state the essentials we wish
to keep, but we must state them clearly.   The majority
of Constable's followers in landscape have failed because they tried to do too many things all at once.
Constable himself, sometimes, as in the finished painting
of the *Haywain*, attempts to blend too many qualities
in a single work.   Hence the large sketch for it at
South Kensington, which attempts much less, is more
powerful, lively and fresh.

We must not only choose our essential features
rightly, but we must take care that there are not too
many of them, or they will nullify one another and the
result will be ineffective.   In a pen and ink sketch, or
an etching, of a sunlit meadow the untouched paper
may be a sufficient symbol of the brightness of the sky
and the grass, but we should risk losing much of this
brilliancy were we to lower the tones by adding colour.
It is for this reason that so few pictures minutely
painted from nature have any liveliness.   They attempt
too much.

Rembrandt's best etchings owe their peculiar power to his self-restraint in this respect. In his early plates he makes effort after effort at rendering local colour. When however experience had shown him that these efforts always resulted in heaviness, he gradually taught himself to do without colour when he needed brilliancy of lighting. As his portraits prove, he could suggest colour magnificently if the occasion required it.

Lastly, the perfect pictorial symbol will suggest life and vigour by the seeming ease and swiftness of its execution. I say *seeming* ease, because an appearance of facility may often have to be attained with great labour, and is generally obtained only by long practice. The fluent sweep of Rubens's brush, the caressing touch of Gainsborough, and the slashing strokes of Sargent, convey alike to the spectator an impression of power and liveliness which enhances immensely the effect of their work, and this faculty of rapid handling is so generally recognised to-day that it has become a fashion with the younger generation of artists, just as the fashion of their seniors is the exact contrary.

Is it always recognised that this swiftness is admissible only in treating essentials, that if these essentials are not grasped by the artist the result is an advertisement of unessentials—in other words a shallow mannerism that has nothing solid behind it? Much of our clever modern portraiture, in which Sargent's facility is aped without a tithe of his power and knowledge, is open to this charge of superficiality, just as the modern landscape, which is founded on imperfect apprehension of Ruskin and the Pre-Raphaelites, inclines to the opposite extreme, dulness.

This clear and swift statement of essentials is a matter of immense consequence in art. Even where, as in the case of etching, the materials employed can render only a few attributes of the object they are employed to interpret, these conditions of clearness and swiftness, if duly observed, will produce a far stronger sense of vitality than an elaborate representation in which the full force of the palette is employed. Has any painter ever invested stone and plaster with the life that breathes from the etched lines of Meryon ?

The paintings and drawings of the Chinese and Japanese masters possess a similar intense vitality, calligraphic as they are; so do the drawings of Rembrandt and Gainsborough. The case of Gainsborough is especially striking, because his convention for drawing such things as trees is hardly less calligraphic than the convention of the Chinese, though it is founded upon a more personal knowledge of nature and, as a generalisation of her infinite detail, is more graceful and less pedantic. Yet though his art is thus conventional and calligraphic, Gainsborough is able, even in a chalk drawing, to convey an impression of the freshness and vitality of landscape no less vivid than that produced by Constable with all his earnest enthusiasm, or by Rubens with his unequalled strength.

In this connection a word must be added on one feature peculiar to modern painting, namely the suggestion of light, atmosphere and movement by broken tones, and separate strokes or spots of pigment. That the vibration of these scattered touches of pigment is in some degree analogous to the vibration of nature's light and nature's air is incontestable, though with not a few this vibration theory has been pushed to the verge of caricature. At present there is a tendency to make a universal formula out of a method that is no more than an additional means of artistic expression applicable only to a limited class of subjects. Hence we see portraits or still-life subjects painted, often cleverly enough, with a technical symbolism that is fit only for the suggestion of twilight, wind or blazing sunshine. The error is one which time will correct in due course, but not before many clever painters have ruined their life's work by reason of it.

III

When, then, we have once decided what the essentials of our subject are, every complexity which diminishes the clearness of the symbol we employ to represent them, every moment that we linger over the strokes we apply to our canvas, must in some degree diminish the vigour of the result we obtain. Were vitality the supreme end of art the artist's task would thus be a simple one. But there are other things to be considered. We have not only to make our work a thing that catches the attention for the moment by its vigour, but something that will hold and enchant the attention by its subtlety.

Our pictorial symbol must thus contain some element of complexity in addition to its directness and swiftness or it will soon appear tedious and empty. So we render to the infinitely varied touch of a Raphael or Watteau the homage we cannot extend to the flourishes of a writing master; so the blotted bistre wash of a Rembrandt or a Claude is pregnant with a mystery that we never find in the flat lithographic tones of Prout and Harding.

It is on this point that the commonly accepted view of good drawing is fallacious. The drawing of Flaxman, for example, will still pass current with many because it is clean and neat and decisive, but how empty and mannered is it seen to be if compared with the infinite variety of the line of Ingres! All Academic teaching since the days of Michelangelo and Raphael has been a failure, because it has condemned students to copy the manner of former masters instead of directing them to look in nature for the subtlety and variety which those masters found there. It has compelled them to part with all sense of life by forcing them to spend weeks over a drawing instead of hours ; to obscure the significant features of the model before them by the addition of a mass of unessential details, and the imitation of minor attributes, such as texture or unimportant variations of local colour.

The one quality which separates the true draughtsman from the clever drawing master, is an intense persistent sympathy with the exquisite refinement of nature's modelling and nature's colour. To cultivate and develop this sympathy by a determined effort to see and delineate subtlety of curvature and surface, even at the cost of all appearance of accomplishment or vigour, should be the first aim of every student. Without it no routine of practice can avert ultimate failure; with it even an unready draughtsman will in time develop competence.

It is here that the need of constant study of nature comes to our help. We can only hope to interpret nature in art by symbols, but those symbols will hardly be symbols of nature at all if they have not something of the infinite variety and subtlety that we find in nature. To inspire our symbols with vitality we must set them down as quickly as we can, yet as we do so we must have ever present in our minds the character and complexity of the things those symbols represent. We must know nature, we must love nature, we must respect nature, all the time we are making use of her. If we ever trust to mere dexterity of hand, mere habit of touch, we fall at once into mannerisms, and our work becomes shallow. Though we may deceive our contemporaries for the moment by an appearance of skill and vigour, we may be sure that posterity will have time to reflect upon our work, will recognise its emptiness, and will relegate us to the oblivion which engulfs impartially the dunce and the man who is merely clever.

IV

So much has already been said about the necessity of Repose in art that its application to pictorial symbols need not detain us long. If our symbols are to be restful we must be careful not to sacrifice everything to vitality; that is the truth of the whole matter. In the matter of tone for example we must beware of excess of contrast, and in making a forcible study with very black chalk we shall achieve a more harmonious result by working on a toned paper than by using one which is dead white. So when using line we must be careful not to avoid tameness and dryness by rushing into the opposite extremes of contortion, as did many Germans of the Renaissance, and many of the Chinese and Japanese artists, or of conceited flourishes as did many of the later Italians. Nor when using colour should we attempt to force it to the loud and noisy pitch many moderns affect, notably the Germans, led away by the powerful talent of Böcklin. Our symbols must indeed have vitality, but they must be reasonable also ; that is to say they must be in harmony with the decorative needs of the work of which they form part. Whatever their individual virtue, unless they take their due place quietly within that work they will be out of place and valueless.

Nor must we forget that Repose is an essential quality of the greatest natural objects. Thus, however much we may wish to emphasise the vitality of a rolling plain, of a chaos of tumbled mountains, or of an angry sea, there must ever, in the midst of all this tempestuous movement, be felt the real stability of the earth, the steadfastness of the mountains, or the vast immobile bulk of the sea, upon which the largest waves that ever swelled are no more than mere momentary froth. It is from this sense of the everlasting unconquerable, immeasurable mass, space, and serenity of nature, and not from the agitations of superficial things such as winds and waters and clouds, that we derive the most profound and majestic impressions. Our art should therefore strive to keep in harmony with nature's repose, or we shall stand but a poor chance of understanding her when she wakes from it.

CHAPTER VI

EMPHASIS OF PLAN

THE surface planning of a picture is all-important. A well planned work with no particular felicity of execution will more than hold its own against the most brilliant feat of brushwork that is based upon a poor design. The labour of planning a composition may appear tedious, but it bears with it a double reward. Not only does it enable us to treat the matter in hand to the best advantage, but the exercise of the eye and the brain, in spacing and placing the essential points of the composition, trains those organs for facing future problems of the same kind. So we may reasonably hope that the designs which, in youth, we make by painful and conscious effort, will in manhood come to our trained perceptions with the swiftness of instinct.

In every visual conception there must be certain cardinal points on which the expression of the subject depends. These we have first to fix, and define to ourselves in their relative order of importance. That is to say we must decide quite finally what is the principal thing we wish to express. If we hesitate, even for a moment, between two rival centres of interest, we shall be wise to lay our design aside until reflection has settled which of them can best be subordinated to the other.

I

We must in fact begin by recognising the pictorial condition of Unity. A good picture has one subject, not two or three subjects; one focus, not several.

Secondly the principal feature will have most prominence if it be placed somewhere near the centre of the composition. To place it actually in the centre is advisable only in formal compositions; or where the effect of formality can be disguised by an unequal disposition of masses elsewhere.

Thirdly its effect will be strengthened and enhanced if it be supported on each side by secondary masses. These may be small or large, but the predominance of the central mass must in some way be preserved. This may frequently be done by making it receive the principal light, or by investing it with special force or distinctness of colour, but so far as plan alone is concerned it is most readily secured by making the focus of the picture rise higher than its supports.

Here we arrive at the principal of triangular or

pyramidal composition; which, however disguised, is the secret of almost all stable and compact pictorial designs. In a portrait the head forms a natural apex to the arms and body. In early religious painting the group of the Madonna and Child naturally takes a pyramidal shape, which in elaborate compositions is disguised by an architectural or landscape setting, and by flanking figures of attendant saints. The apex of the pyramid is often balanced below the base by the introduction of some smaller feature of interest, which serves as a new link to tie the flanking masses together, so that the triangle becomes a quadilateral.

With Raphael this quadilateral or diamond shaped plan is further disguised by softening and rounding the enclosing lines until the pattern becomes an oval. This oval in its turn is supplemented in his most elaborate designs, such as the *Disputá* and *Transfiguration*, by a triangular mass being arranged below it, so that the composition consists of two systems instead of one.

The oval is often used alone by bad landscape painters, and is often recommended to amateurs as a safe and easy system of arrangement. Like its relative the vignette, the oval lacks the firm lines that make for power. Claude, Turner and Corot alike are seen to the least advantage in the compositions by them that are based on this feeble system.

In Venice Giorgione, and Titian after him, introduced

new modifications of the pyramid. Romantic suggestion rather than majestic statement was their aim and, to admit the feeling of uncertainty which they needed, they were compelled to get rid of the restful obvious firmness of the pyramidal arrangement, or at least to disguise it. In Giorgione's *Fête Champêtre* in the Louvre, the group to the right is composed in the traditional way, the summits of the house and the tallest tree behind it accenting and repeating its pyramidal form, but the figure turning to the fountain, while harmonising with the seated figures, leads the eye away from them in an upward sweep to the left, and so prevents their formality from striking the eye. In the so-called *Sacred and Profane Love* in the Borghese Gallery, Titian goes still further, for the two chief figures, and the sarcophagus on which they lean, form the base and sides of a pyramid whose apex we cannot see, for it is outside and above the picture.

With Veronese, Tintoret, Rubens and the decorative painters who followed in their footsteps, movement and variety came into fashion in the place of Unity, so that the crowded compositions of these painters are no longer openly based upon the solid and stable form of the pyramid. In all simpler designs, however, it may still be traced, though it is frequently disguised by devices such as those invented by Giorgione and Titian, or by the introduction of two or more intersecting pyramids into the same picture. This method will be found to explain many designs which, like the colour prints of Hokusai, at first sight seem too capricious or too complicated for analysis.

Indeed when once the pyramidal idea of composition is thoroughly grasped, few stable and coherent designs are found to be without it. Canaletto's canals and Claude's sea-pieces resolve themselves into schemes of two pyramids, a greater and a less placed side by side, even when we do not find in the centre a smaller repetition of the form making the focus of interest, as in Claude's *Seaport* (No. 14) in the National Gallery.

II

Yet vitality, the sense of life and movement, is for many subjects as important or even more important than absolute coherence. How then when we wish to give vitality to our work can we emphasise it in the arrangement of the ground plan ?

Ideas of motion are most forcibly suggested to us by those sharp oppositions of diagonal lines which we note in the movements of the larger animals, or in the spiral undulating curves of a flame. It is with such lines as these that we must work if we are to get the appearance of life and motion.

In Rubens and Tintoret we see violent and turbulent action suggested by the rapid involution of the curves of the figures and draperies, sharply contrasted here and there with the rigid lines of weapons or architecture. In the pastoral compositions of Claude and Corot, as in the gentle Madonnas of Raphael, the curves have a more suave undulation and are much less abruptly opposed by rigid lines. Where these curves are broken by too many smaller modulations, as in the work of many eclectic artists, the effect becomes restless and weak.

If we can balance the significant lines by a repetition or echo, their emphasis will be enhanced and the rhythmic quality of the design much improved.

The nature of rhythm, although it lies at the root of all decorative design, has never been studied in relation to painting so methodically as it has been analysed in connection with poetry. In poetry we recognise at once how the obvious periodic recurrence of certain accented syllables, which we term metre, plays a most important part in determining the character of any particular poem. We cannot write an epic in hendeca-syllables, nor a love song in the metre of " Dies Irae."

So in painting, the character of a design is determined by its general pattern. The stern contours of a Poussin will not fit the themes of a Fragonard, any better than the style of Cosway would have suited William Blake. Each subject with which the painter has to deal has thus a class of patterns corresponding to it, from which

E

the painter must choose if he is to present his matter effectively.

We may take a second hint from poetry as to the limits within which this condition applies. While the general character of a poem is to some considerable extent dominated by the metre employed, its quality is determined not only by the intrinsic value of its subject-matter, but by the way in which the metre emphasises or accents that value.

We have thus, as it were, two kinds of rhythm. One is the formal metre of the poem which governs its general character; the other the delicate adaptation of the metrical accent to the particular thoughts which the poem conveys. So in painting, we have to consider not only the large and obvious sweep of the main lines and masses, but also the subordinate rhythmical quality of the component elements. In the work of an imperfectly trained artist, such as William Blake, we may find the main disposition of the pattern to be grand and appropriate, but the minor rhythms to be mannered and conventional. Such work might be described as possessing more character than quality: while the pictures of the minor Dutch painters where, if the details are ingenious, the general plan is petty and confused, might be described as possessing more quality than character.

We have seen that rhythm implies periodic recurrence or repetition. If that repetition is definite and apparent, it will, like rhyme in poetry, make for a corresponding directness of emphasis. If the character of the primary rhythm be lively, repetition will enhance its vitality; if it be restful, repetition will enhance its repose. Cotman's *Wherries on the Yare*, where the sweep of the great sail is echoed by the cloud forms behind it, is a striking example of the simple and forcible patterns which may thus be obtained.

If the recurrence is too frequent and too regular, the result will be pettiness with a bad painter, artificiality or confusion with a good one. Rubens for instance, from sheer exuberance of spirits, has a tendency to repeat flowing curves till his figures seem to writhe rather than to move. An ill-designed wall-paper, for a similar reason, may often be singularly irritating; nor can a very short definite metre be used for a very long poem without becoming tiresome.

On the other hand recurrences which are slightly irregular, and which suggest the primary rhythm without exactly imitating it, will usually be pleasurable. So the finest poetry is not that which conforms uniformly and exactly to metrical stress, but that in which metre is most subtly and infinitely varied in accordance with the thought expressed. Yet this desire for subtlety must not be carried too far, or we shall obscure the main rhythm and so lose infinitely more in character than we gain by polish. The cultured modern poet may dull his talent thus : our younger painters, perhaps, go too far in the opposite direction.

We may note also that symmetrical rhythms, such as those found in early altar-pieces, convey a sense of order, unity, and restfulness ; unsymmetrical rhythms, as we shall see, may convey a sense of movement.

Hogarth in his almost forgotten treatise, "The Analysis of Beauty," has devoted some space to considering in what precise form of curve the most perfect beauty resides, midway between the swelling curves which are pompous and extravagant, and the flatter ones which produce an effect of stiffness. In its immediate and practical bearing on picture-making the discussion is of small importance.

To propose any definite geometrical curve, as containing in itself a line of perfect beauty, is as futile as to impose upon the artist any rigid canon of the human form. As we saw in the Introduction, canons of correct proportions have often been studied, and formulæ for them have been worked out, even by great artists. But no great artist has ever allowed his powers of expression to be hampered by such a formula, or has employed it except as a convenient mean from which a significant deviation could start. The great Greek sculptors from whom our modern canons are usually derived, did just the same, each proving his originality by deviating from the canons of his predecessors in search of a new and slightly different type of human perfection. It is

just as absurd to search after a single ideal contour, as it
is to suppose that some single ideal human form exists
which is equally appropriate to all subjects and conditions of treatment.

Hogarth's general principle of the use of spiral,
serpentine, or flame-like lines to suggest vitality and
motion will, in fact, be more serviceable to the painter
than the too rigid formula for the curve itself which he
grafted upon it. In practice we find curves of very
different kinds associated in the same picture, those
that approach the stiffness of a straight line tending to
austerity of effect, those with a more undulating flow
suggesting more lively motion.

The upright and horizontal lines of Hobbema's
famous *Avenue* would make the picture seem stiff and
rigid but for the sweeping curves of the cumulus clouds
above them. Piero della Francesca's *Baptism* is even
more formal, the one concession to the element of
vitality being made up of the spiral line formed by the
curve of the river, the back of the figure stripping his
shirt, the sweep of the hill-side and the rounded
masses of foliage on the left, assisted by the arched
top of the panel.

In Botticelli's *Nativity* a much greater degree of
vitality is suggested by the exquisitely interlaced lines
of the various groups, to which the rectilinear forms of
the manger and the trees behind give a note of dignity.
The pattern of this picture might well be compared

with Blake's glorious design of *The Morning Stars.*
The still more fierce and full-blooded vitality of Titian's
Bacchus and Ariadne is emphasised by the presence of
spirals everywhere, while the level lines of the sea and
the clouds, with the vertical lines of the tree trunks,
just serve to keep the effect from being tumultuous, as
we sometimes find it in Correggio or Rubens, and often
in the works of the Italian and Flemish eclectics,
whose sprawling saints and fluttering angels are now
so odious in our eyes.

We must note, too, how the placing of the chief
mass of a picture may suggest motion, and that in a
particular direction. In a portrait, for example, if the
figure be placed near one side of the frame, it will often
seem to be moving into or out of the picture space,
according to the direction in which the head is turned.
If the head looks away from the centre, the figure will
appear to be retiring; if the head turns towards the
centre, the figure will seem to be advancing into the
picture. Even the turn of the body will sometimes be
enough, as Romney's admirable half-length of *Lady
Hamilton with a Goat* indicates.

A similar massing of the figures within a diagonal
drawn from corner to corner accentuates the swing and
movement of Titian's *Europa*, now unfortunately lost to
England. This form of design is commonly used by
landscape painters to emphasise effects of wind and
storm: the wind seeming to blow out of the picture

towards the side where the masses are heaped up within the diagonal. The drawings and etchings of Legros include many examples of this kind of emphasis.

III

Infinity perhaps depends less upon planning than upon the subsequent stages of picture-making, yet even the plan of a picture may sometimes assist materially in producing this effect. It does so by giving to the mere general aspect of a picture an elusive quality, which at once attracts the eye and defies analysis, whether by subtle complexity of parts as in Titian's *Bacchus and Ariadne*, in Turner's *Calais Pier*, and Rubens's *Chateau de Stein*, or by an equally subtle simplicity which disguises the artifices used to produce it, as in Rembrandt's *Landscape with Tobias and the Angel*, Turner's *Bligh Sands*, and Crome's *Windmill*. Where the artifice of the design is apparent, as in Fra Bartolommeo's *Holy Family*, this quality is lost at once, and even Gainsborough's splendid gifts as a painter, a colourist, and a poet, never quite compensate for the obvious arrangement on which *The Market Cart* is based.

So far as infinity of plan is concerned, it would seem as if the artist ought first to arrange his subjects with the utmost skill he possesses, and then use still more care in removing or disguising all traces of his previous deliberation. Painters are but novices in their craft who compose pictures of which the secret can be . exhausted at once.

IV

As ideas of motion are conveyed by diagonal or spiral lines, so ideas of repose are conveyed by vertical or horizontal lines. A level expanse of calm water, or the upright shaft of a poplar on a windless day, of themselves convey the idea of repose to us; while in a place of tumbled rocks and mountains, be the day never so still, our minds are affected by the sense of movement.

If then our design is wholly made up of swelling and diagonal lines it will be restless, and though restless-ness may be the feeling which we wish to state emphatically, we must not forget that we have to state it within the limits of the conditions proper to paint-ing. Now since a picture is liable to be seen constantly, any restlessness of design tends to become more and more evident with the lapse of time, and the spectator's discomfort will increase with the scale of the picture, and the pitch of its tone. Many of the large and elaborate works of the Bolognese School are un-pleasing to us on this account. If they were painted on a small scale and with less force of tone and colour their defects would not be so importunate. When re-produced as book illustrations, and so seen but intermittently, they may not trouble us at all, and may make us wonder why we like tne originals so little.

The ideas of repose which we connect with horizontal and vertical lines are strengthened when the lines are repeated, as in the case of the level flakes of cloud in a sunset sky, but specially so when the repetition is made with symmetry or order, as in the façade of a Greek temple, or the rows of columns in a church. Architecture indeed is the most readily accessible means of introducing an element of repose into a composition. So generally has this been recognised that nearly all good decorative paintings, from classical times to our own day, have an architectural setting or an architectural background. Where architecture is absent, vertical re-flection in water that is still or nearly so, the level horizons formed by the sea or by a distant plain, serve a similar purpose. The work of the Italian painters of the fifteenth century will suggest countless examples.

One form of figure composition, however, must be mentioned which gets the effect of repose, of order and succession, out of the figures themselves. It may be termed processional composition, and may be illustrated by the long rows of standing saints who make such splendid decoration in S. Apollinare Nuovo at Ravenna, by the groups of upright figures in the frescoes of Giotto, Angelico and other great early Italian Masters, by the tall ladies who walk side by side in the prints of Kiyonaga and Outamaro, or by the *Entombment* as etched by Rembrandt or painted by Blake. Among modern masters, Rossetti and Burne Jones have used it the most freely and effectively in England, and Puvis de Chavannes in France.

A very small proportion of vertical and horizontal lines is quite enough to give an effect of repose to any picture of moderate size, and it is often far better to get repose in this way, than to get it by diluting the colour scheme or by weakening contrasts of light and shade. The use of a more or less symmetrical plan, as we have already seen, will also assist this effect of order and restfulness.

The most dangerous of all methods, however, of aiming at repose is by rounding off masses and edges, and generally substituting gentle curves for square and firm shapes. Stiffness and angularity, it is true, are not pleasant qualities in art, yet they have a certain manly strength and vigour, while the softness which comes of too much rounding off corners, and too much searching for grace and suavity, is but a bastard and meretricious quality that leads inevitably to the repose of languor, emptiness and impotence, instead of to the nobler repose that implies strength kept well in hand.

When therefore we read of egg-shaped and elliptical compositions, even though they be backed with such names as Claude and Turner and Corot, we must never forget that the effect of these designs, where it happens to be fine, depends on the rectilinear forms they contain and not upon their sweeping curves. It is because Claude had not time to work out these curves in his sketches from nature that his sketches are so generally superior to his finished paintings. Turner's fondness for architecture saves him again and again from the same form of weakness, and Corot's best designs are those which have the most straight lines in them.

In figure painting Raphael was the fatal example, although, in almost all that he did with his own hand, the rounded curves of the figures and the draperies are contrasted with level ground, upright trees or architecture. It is from want of this contrast of straight lines that the celestial figures in the *Transfiguration* look as if they were dancing. For the same reason Parmigiano's large altar-piece in the National Gallery looks empty and artificial.

That a certain degree of suavity and grace is pleasurable in pictorial design no one would be austere enough to deny. Yet to search for it, or to encourage it, seems to be a dangerous habit that grows with use, and has ruined many masters of great original talent. The peril is the more insidious because suavity seems to become a trick of hand, by which the brush works in a series of fluent connected sweeps, while the brain and the eye, even in the presence of nature, remain idle.

The etchings of Rembrandt, if examined chronologically, are a striking illustration of the way in which that great master gradually shook himself free from the rounded designs he had learned from his early teachers, and adopted the architectural schemes on which the great plates of his maturity are constructed. If we also can keep the main lines of our compositions architectural in character, we shall at least be on the safe side so far as the quality of repose is concerned.

CHAPTER VII

EMPHASIS OF SPACING

THE general surface arrangement of a picture having been discussed, we have now to consider what the relative measurements of the parts should be, and what proportion each should bear to the whole composition. If the reasonableness of a painting may be said to depend upon its general plan, its decorative effect may to a large extent be considered as dependent upon its spacing. Yet spacing is one of the qualities ot which only a small proportion of our painters seem to think, in spite of the recent example of Whistler. The best living masters of the art of spacing are a few painters who have designed posters, and the equally small body which bases its efforts upon study of the great Italians* and the great Dutchmen.

We may note here that, quite apart from the relative spacing of the masses inside a picture, we have also to consider the space which the picture itself must

* Mr. Berenson's well-known handbook on "The Central Italian Painters of the Renaissance ' contains an illuminating study of the talent of the Umbrian masters for this " space-composition."

cover in order to do perfect justice to its subject. A small reproduction of a large composition like Raphael's *Parnassus,* however accurate, will never have the breadth and dignity of the original. Raphael's exquisite little *Vision of a Knight,* on the other hand, would look empty were it enlarged to life size. We feel instinctively that the scale of Chardin and Terboich, of De Hooghe and Vermeer and Metsu, suits their modest *genre,* far better than the life size scale of a Spanish *bodegone* piece (even if it be by Velasquez himself), of our modern Royal Academy realism, or of the Scotch followers of Whistler.

If certain subjects are so great that even a vast wall is not too large for their adequate treatment, we may be tolerably sure that the artists who are strong enough to conceive such things will also be wise enough to know how they must be painted. In the present day for one picture that might well have been painted on a large canvas, a hundred, nay a thousand are produced which would look infinitely better if they were a quarter of their present size. Exhibition rivalry and (though the lesson of the auction room is the exact contrary) the popular confusion of size with value, are no doubt largely responsible for this megalomania; but are -painters really any more to blame than authors or politicians for risking vacuity to obtain advertisement ?

There can be no real doubt as to the scale into which the true artist will cast his sword. The compressing of much matter into a small canvas, if a fault, is a venial fault compared with its opposite—working on too large a scale—which must inevitably result in dilution, weakness, and vacancy. There are few subjects for which a single square yard of canvas in the hands of a master is not enough ; among those chosen by modern artists there are fewer still for which one or two square feet would not be ample.

I

Unity can be secured by spacing only in one way— namely by providing that the prominent spaces or masses in a picture are not exactly equal. In processional compositions indeed, the separate figures may be of about equal importance, but the real question of spacing that is involved in such designs is one of the relative proportion between the figures taken all together and their background.

The spacing of a picture then must always be so arranged that we cannot be in doubt as to which is the principal mass and which are the subordinate ones. By the masters of the sixteenth, seventeenth, and eighteenth centuries this argument was extended mathematically to the subordinate masses, so that painters had not only a primary and predominant light but also a second, a third, a fourth and a fifth in a regular sequence of diminishing importance. The idea, may be theoretically correct, but in practice it hampers talent. The mere effort to make pictures conform to such a rule as this must deprive them of freshness and naturalness, and these are really of more importance than any minor details. Such things may well be left to good taste. The great thing is to get the main divisions of a picture settled in the way which suits the subject-matter best.

There are several recipes to this end with which students can experiment, especially in such comparatively simple matters as the place to be occupied by the horizon, or the skyline which in most out-door subjects determines the broad divisions of light and dark. Artists often place the horizon one third of the way up the picture, thus giving the sky two thirds of the space, and the ground one third. Such a rule would be more generally useful if horizons were always flat, and were unbroken by objects or figures rising above them.

In practice the irregular shape of the masses and, frequently, the indeterminate nature of their outlines, makes any mechanical measurement of such proportion impossible. We are driven at last to judge of the relative size of the masses by the eye alone, and only by constant practice and observation can we train our vision to avoid instinctively the awkward results produced by equality of mass. The fault often steals upon us insidiously. A very slight alteration in working

from an effective sketch, is quite enough to destroy the
balance of parts on which the effect depended, and to
make the finished picture an undecided thing, at which
we have to look again and again before being able to
discover which is the real dominant quantity.

II

Directly this question becomes possible the picture is
in some degree imperfect, for it has lost the sense of
vitality which is communicated to us by a forcible and
striking statement. If the spacing of a picture is to be
thus striking and forcible, it must not only be definite
in character but must have in it some element of the
unusual. The works of the artists of China and Japan are
full of examples of such novel disposition. Frequently
indeed, it is carried by them to lengths which seem to
us fantastic or capricious, yet in no other works perhaps
is vitality so constantly and so powerfully felt. In the
same way, the works of Goya, which are among the
most lively of European productions, are also among
the most capriciously spaced.

Pleasure in such bold spacing prevents us from
thinking Hobbema's *Avenue* to be formal, or De Hooch's
Dutch courtyards to be tame: it gives distinction to
Crome's *Windmill*, and enlarges the little *Crucifixion* by
Andrea dal Castagno to heroic dimensions. Mantegna

F

and Rembrandt, Veronese and Tiepolo afford numerous examples of how this form of emphasis may be nobly employed.

Perhaps, however, its effects are most noticeable in the works of men whose other gifts are moderate, but who rise, in virtue of this single quality, to something like real greatness, as Perugino does in his best works, such as the fresco in Sta. Maria Maddalena de' Pazzi. Indeed, when a subject is in itself somewhat tame, a proper use of forcible spacing is perhaps the best of all devices for turning it into a good picture. The works of Whistler show how little material is really needed to make a fine work of art, provided only that the spacing is well and boldly planned. Watts's noble picture of *Jacob and Esau* enforces the same lesson. Here we have only two figures meeting in an empty landscape, but so deftly are they placed within the picture space, so grandly do they dominate the horizon, that we are compelled to recognise at once that this is no ordinary meeting, and that the personages are no ordinary men. The works of Millet and Puvis de Chavannes might also be instanced.

The general absence of this quality is one of the causes which make the work of the seventeenth-century eclectic schools seem so dull and lifeless, and gives, by contrast, such charm to an occasional exception, like Andrea Sacchi's *Vision of St. Romuald* in the Vatican.

Paintings with the intense ubiquitous vigour of a Rubens do not of course stand in need of much assistance from spacing, but when a painter's sense of vitality is not strong, as with Claude when painting in oil, he cannot dispense with bold spacing without incurring the reproach of tameness. Claude, to do him justice, spaces his admirable drawings with singular freedom, and so preserves in them a life and freshness that are rarely seen in his oil pictures.

III

The proportion of the masses in a picture must not only be unusual and striking. It must also be subtle, so that the ratio of the masses to each other is not readily apprehended by the eye.

To divide a picture into two equal halves, either horizontally or vertically, is recognised as absurd even by beginners. Yet in text-books on art it is not uncommon to find recommendation of the principle we have mentioned, of placing the horizon in a landscape at one third of the total height of the canvas. A rule which leaves the two chief masses, the earth and the sky, in such an easily recognised proportion as $1:2$ seems only a stage removed from equal division· Proportions less readily measured by the eye, such as $2:3$ or $3:4$, would be infinitely better ; indeed the latter is very frequently used by good composers

The question resolves itself in the end, like most other questions of the kind, into one of fitness. The solution of each problem in proportion is determined by the particular kind of pictorial emphasis that the subject and the occasion demand.

Those who find themselves interested by the subject, may speculate as to the significance of the cryptic phrase with which the saying attributed to Michelangelo concludes, " a figure should be pyramidal, serpentine, and *multiplied by one two and three*." Hogarth after quoting the last words and referring to their importance, omits to give any explanation of their meaning. Probably the study of fine examples of architecture would, in practice, be more advantageous than abstract mathematical inquiry, for there measurement is easy, and the question is not complicated by the irregularities of contour which, in the case of painting, often render the use of a foot-rule impossible. The student of the subject may be encouraged by the fact that the great masters without exception developed this faculty gradually, and that their late works are almost uniformly more subtle in their proportions than are their early ones.

The common practice of surrounding a sketch with pieces of paper, and noting the changes effected by shifting them so that the proportions are continually altered, can be strongly recommended as a simple means of training the eye. Incidentally too, it will prove that there is no single formula for spacing, but that each effect has its own appropriate set of proportions.

IV

The element of repose in spacing is more easily dealt with. Repose may be obtained by leaving a certain portion of the picture space blank, or nearly blank. The larger the space so left, the more quiet and restful will the spirit of the work become. With the earlier masters both of Italy and Flanders this quiet is usually secured by a background of tranquil sky. Velasquez carries the search for repose to an extreme point, so that not only have his portraits a simple setting of floor and empty wall, but even the figures themselves are as flatly and broadly treated as possible. Hence comes the air of gravity by which his portraits are distinguished. Where turbulence is aimed at, as in many of Rubens's figure subjects, the empty spaces vanish. The methods of Constable and Whistler show a similar contrast. In the landscapes of Constable, the fitful movements of the wind and flickering sunlight require for their suggestion the filling of every inch of the picture with spots of detail; the tranquil effects of Whistler demand a large preponderance of almost vacant space.

We must beware, however, in trying to obtain repose, lest we dilute our spacing till the effect becomes empty. Every design has a scale that suits it exactly. If carried out on a smaller scale it will seem confined and compressed ; if carried out on a larger scale it will seem thin and vacuous. Of the two faults the former is commonly the less hurtful, in that it does suggest a certain pleasurable fulness of content, quite apart from such advantages as portability. A design carried out on too large a scale may be restful but, if it is also empty and cumbrous, and perhaps executed with the coarseness of touch which a large scale encourages, its merits have been gained by too heavy a sacrifice.

CHAPTER VIII

EMPHASIS OF RECESSION

WE have hitherto discussed the position of the masses of a picture so far as they affect its surface planning. We have now to consider their arrangement in the world created by the picture; the relative distance from the eye which each is intended to suggest, and the system on which this fictitious recession can be disposed. The subject was much studied in the past by painters who had to deal with a number of figures, since it was universally recognised that absence of plan led to confusion, and the simple placing of all the figures on the same plane tended to archaic stiffness. The principles of this kind of arrangement are however so closely related to those of the general planning of a picture that they do not call for lengthy discussion.

I

The space represented within the four sides of a picture frame or mount may, for practical purposes, be compared to a long room which we see from a window at one end. The effect of perspective causes all lines at right angles to the plane of our vision to tend to meet at the centre of the horizon opposite to us, as the cornices and skirting boards of our imaginary room would do. We have only to imagine the room of great height, width, and infinite length to see that the walls, the ceiling, and the floor will form triangles with a common apex. In painting we have to work as if the walls of this imaginary room were made of glass, and we could see a certain distance outside them, but the objects immediately in front of our picture foreground will recede in the same triangular form as that assumed by the floor of our room when seen in perspective.

If then we desire to secure the greatest possible effect of unity in a picture, we shall see that the objects it represents are arranged on some such triangular plan. It does not matter much how irregular the triangle is ; its sides may be curved into a semi-circle, or further, extended to form an ellipse, the principle remains the same. If one side be developed fully, as it would be if we were painting a range of mountains retiring in perspective, or a view along the edge of a wood, or the side of a row of buildings, a very small object on the opposite side of the picture will give the needed balance and complete our imaginary triangle.

The great thing is to avoid the doubling of the triangle, by an arrangement which leads the eye inwards to two separate points. We are then placed like a spectator at the angle where two galleries meet, who can look down both of them. In practical life such a position is often serviceable; in pictures it leads to a division of interest which is just the reverse.

A word may be added as to the place of the principal object in such a scheme. In landscape this is frequently in the distance or mid-distance, although a prominent object in the foreground, such as a tree, may serve as a *repoussoir*, to give relief to things farther away and to provide the real focus of interest with some support or counterpoise. Yet this *repoussoir* must not be too attractive. A ship for example, if painted with any care, is so complicated and so interesting an object that if placed near the foreground it is apt to become the principal feature of the composition, while the background, however intrinsically interesting, takes second place. In sea-pieces ships, when placed near the foreground, are commonly made the chief subject, while when we come to foreground figures, the interest of which is greater still than that of ships, the background tends to become even more subordinate. In a figure-piece then the figures may naturally occupy the foreground and, however forcibly we paint the objects behind them, the figures will rarely lose their predominance.

The greatest difficulty of treating these problems of recession occurs in landscape. There the main subject is frequently the distance and, if the tones of it are at all delicate, we have to be specially careful not to crush them by a too forcible or interesting foreground. It is for this reason that sketches, in which the foreground is left unfinished, are so generally superior in effect to the most highly finished pictures.

II

Yet if taken too literally this principle of triangular recession would give us very stiff and formal arrangements. To endow it with life it must be varied by serpentine or undulating lines. The objects in a picture will thus have a tendency to recede with alternate movements to this side or that, as do the indented flanks of a mountain, the lines of a winding road, or the curves of a river.

The work of Raphael in its various stages will serve to illustrate the development of these modes of recession. In his earlier works, such as the *Vision of a Knight* and the *Ansidei Madonna* in the National Gallery, the figures are placed side by side as in the pictures of his master Perugino. When on coming to Rome he had to group a large number of figures for the first time, as in the *Disputà*, they are arranged in the form of semi-circles receding from the spectator. In the later frescoes, such as the *School of Athens* and the *Expulsion of Heliodorus*, this general form is still preserved, but is concealed by an artful irregularity in the disposition of the groups, all of which deviate on one side or another from a regular geometrical plan. The *Disputà* in consequence has a somewhat formal look, in comparison with the movement and vitality suggested by the undulating ground plan of these later frescoes.

It is chiefly however in large decorative works, containing numerous figures, that artifice has to be used thus deliberately. In pictures of average size the chief objects or figures are not numerous and, in landscape especially, may be widely separated; yet they must be arranged with as much system as if they were really connected by subordinate groups. The placing of the ships, boats, and buoys in Turner's sea-pieces will illustrate in how many pleasant ways the eye may be led away from the foreground by the alternate disposition of isolated objects, no two of which are at the same distance from the eye, or fail to suggest by their relation to their neighbours the sinuous curves from which we derive the sense of vitality

III

The sense of infinity, so far as the arrangement of the planes of recession is concerned, is conveyed by the subtle artifices, the variations from strict rule, by which the general plan is enriched and concealed.

The minor painters of Holland often fail in this matter They arrange their figures and pots and pans with such admirable system that they are always quoted as examples to students, because their methods are so obvious. Now it is just in escaping from this appearance of deliberate arrangement that the merit of a great artist shows. A composition by De Hooch for example is admirably planned, but the things and persons of which it is made up all seem to have come together of themselves, and to have been caught by the artist in an instant of felicitous conjunction.

A comparison of Rembrandt's later paintings and etchings with those of his early years, indicates with how much labour he freed himself from the artificial completeness of his earlier designs, and how the profundity of his insight developed in exact ratio with his emancipation. The landscape work of Hokusai excels that of the more realistic Hiroshige for just the same reason [quite apart from its immense imaginative and executive superiority], the schemes on which it is framed being more deftly concealed.

In the case of the painters of the English School, it might be pointed out how the rich shadows of Reynolds, the broken touch of Gainsborough, the drifting mists of Turner, and the flickering lights of Constable, all in their respective ways and degrees, enable the artists who employ them to disguise the plan of their pictures, and thereby to give them that sense of mystery and infinity to which a great part of their attractiveness is due. The extraordinary minuteness of certain Pre-Raphaelite pictures, and the vibrant atmosphere of the best Impressionist work have a similar effect, but ordinary modern pictures which are either precise without overwhelming wealth of detail, or rough without really possessing the power of suggesting air and light, miss this sense of infinity altogether.

In portraits and figure-pieces the effect of infinite space is much influenced by the quality of the background, mysterious recession and atmosphere being suggested by broken tones and vibrant quality in the paint. In landscape spaciousness is still more important, and much of the good landscape of the world thus resolves itself into a sky and a distance, supported or relieved by some sort of a foreground. This foreground, as we have said, is always a source of difficulty, and some artists, like Corot, have evaded its tendency to obtrusiveness, by including in their pictures nothing that was less than two or three hundred yards away from their easels. This device might possibly be extended. Many of the most delightful landscapes in the world are to be found in the backgrounds of figure-paintings by the old masters, and these landscapes lose none of their charm when isolated from their setting. It is conceivable that a painter might take a hint from these works, and experiment with landscapes in which what would be the middle distance for other painters was used as a foreground. As the middle

distance and distance of a landscape usually contain its ⌐
most exquisite and mysterious colouring, such a
practice might, in capable hands, produce many novel
and enchanting effects.

IV

Repose of interior plan, like repose of surface plan,
seems to depend largely upon the presence of horizontal or vertical surfaces in the area included by the
picture. These surfaces need not be large in extent if
the position they occupy is a prominent one, and the
other masses of the picture are not tumultuous in
character. The *Conversion of St. Bavon* by Rubens
in the National Gallery is as vigorous and mobile in
design and execution as almost any picture could be,
yet the introduction of a comparatively small mass of
architecture in the background is enough to prevent
the effect from being violent, while the impression
left by such *tours de force* as his *Fall of the Damned* at
Munich is unpleasant simply because we see a mass of
huddled figures without any such background to serve
as a relief. The Venetian masters were specially
fortunate in their use of architecture, or the level
surface of a great plain, or of the sea, as a foil to their
richly clad figures. Rembrandt's large etching, *Christ
presented to the People*, and the works of the great Dutch
painters of interiors, show that an almost empty wall
may be used in just the same way.

CHAPTER IX

EMPHASIS OF SHADOW

THE arrangement of the light and dark masses in a
picture will be governed by the same laws whether we
use shadow, as European artists have done ever since
the fifteenth century, to express the relief, the modelling, the thickness and solidity of things ; or whether
we dispense with shadow, as Oriental artists in general
have done, and regard nature as a mosaic of flat
patches of colour. It is in the matter of representation, rather than in that of composition, that the two
methods differ.

All pictures may be broadly divided into masses of
light, of middle tint, and of shadow. We may not always
be able to distinguish the exact point where these pass
into one another, but we can map them out approximately, and so gain a tolerably accurate record of their
arrangement in any particular work.

This arrangement is a thing of the highest importance. It is this broad pattern of light and dark
masses that first strikes the eye when we look at
a picture, and those who have to look at many pictures

learn to rely upon this pattern as an almost infallible test of pictorial merit, long before the subject, treatment, and details can be clearly apprehended.

I

For this patchwork of light and dark masses to have unity its constituents must blend into a single mass. That mass may be full of complicated details but, it any portion of it stands out so prominently from the rest as to look like a blot or stain upon the picture, the work is at fault.

Again, if the light and shade are so massed that the picture seems to be divided into two nearly equal halves, and the eye cannot readily settle which is the dominant half, the effect of unity has once more been missed, and the work is at fault.

The first of these conditions may be termed unity of tone, the second unity of mass.

It is clear that unity of tone will be most readily produced in pictures where the prevailing tone is one of middle tint, upon which neither extreme of light or darkness can tell as a spot.

Where the prevailing tone tends to be light, the high lights may be forced as much as the artist pleases, they will never tell as definite spots. Dark masses, on the other hand, will stand out sharply from the light ground, and will have to be most carefully placed and blended with it, to prevent them from looking like blots or patches.

The fresco paintings of the early cinquecento masters, or the work of Puvis de Chavannes, will give countless examples of the successful use of a light key without the contrast of strong masses of dark colour. A light key indeed is almost a necessity in true decorative painting.

Further, as easel pictures increase in size, they approach the condition of mural painting and must therefore be governed by similar laws. A large easel picture, then, needs to be lighter in key than a small one, and should contain less forcible oppositions of dark masses, if its effect is to be pleasant.

The practice of painting easel pictures in a light key was the custom from the earliest ages until the use of oil painting became general and painters were fascinated by its deep transparent shadows. Then for some centuries pictures showed a preponderance of middle tint or of darkness, until the art of using oils in a light key was invented by Rubens and Claude and carried to completion by Turner.

In the brilliant key of his mature style, even Turner's darks are apt to tell as spots, although in arranging them, and in blending them with the ground, he displays consummate skill. The Impressionists avoid the difficulty by having no darks at all; but, as paintings pure and simple, their works lack the variety and

G

force of Turner's glowing canvases, for this very reason.

In a sketch, the placing of the dark masses and the fusing of them with the picture scheme should not give any serious trouble; but in a large easel picture where the general tone is light, the treatment of the contrasting points of darkness calls for no little care and experience. On a very large scale, even the deepest darks will have to be of but moderate intensity; on a small scale, a very sharp contrast need not be unpleasant. Tintoret's great *Paradise* in the Ducal Palace would cease to be spotty and confused were its darkest tones of half their present intensity: in a little etching by Rembrandt, the most vigorous opposition of rich black ink to white paper does not irritate the eye.

Conversely, when the general tone of a picture is dark, the lights will show strongly. To preserve unity we must be careful that they blend with the ground, and are carefully placed and proportioned. Any light which does not at some point blend softly with the ground will attract the eye by telling as a spot. Such sharp lights should therefore appear, if at all, close to the focus of interest, as when white linen flashes out close to the head of a portrait.

A sharp light in any other part of the picture will distract the attention, and so should only be used with the definite purpose of balancing a more powerful light, which would otherwise seem isolated. Where for instance a strong light is concentrated upon the head of a portrait, a touch of sharp light on a cuff, or on a paper held in the hand, will prevent the head from being in theatrical isolation.

To render this balance successful such subsidiary lights must be carefully placed ; they must also be carefully proportioned, both in number and extent, to the size of the picture and the feeling it is intended to convey. If they are small and numerous the effect will be spotty ; if they are few and considerable they may compete with the principal mass of light, and the result will be confusion. The eclectic masters of the seventeenth century will provide a sufficiency of examples of failure from these causes. The portraits of Van Dyck or of Reynolds on the other hand might be quoted to illustrate the numerous ways in which success may be attained.

In a picture where the prevailing tone is neither dark nor light both high lights and darks will tell with moderate effect, each fusing somewhat easily with the ground. The use of a dominant middle tint may therefore be serviceable where the subject itself tends to be rather disconnected, as in complicated figure pieces, and in certain types of landscape. The pictures and drawings of Gainsborough will serve as examples.

When there is but little middle tint the picture will consist of two rather strongly contrasted tones, and the effect will tend to be spotty if the masses are numerous, empty if they are few. If darkness predominates the effect will be heavy: if light predominates the effect will be weak. The general remedy in such cases would seem to be the reduction of the contrasts until the picture, as a whole, tells as middle tint. If this tint inclines to be light, as it may do in pictures where an effect of luminosity is required, even sharp lights will blend easily with the ground, and the chief question will be the management of the shadows. If the tint inclines to be dark, the shadows will prove easy to manage, but the lights will need special care.

The one thing necessary is to fuse light and shade and middle tint into a homogeneous mass. An instructive method of study is to examine the development of a line engraving through a series of trial proofs, such as may frequently be found in good print collections. To landscape painters the prints after Turner's drawings should be specially instructive. There we can see the reproduction begin with a bare statement of broad masses, hard at the edge and without any detail, and watch stage by stage the addition of the gradations, half-tones and refinements, by which the effect is gradually softened, enriched and perfected.

II

Vitality may be very effectively suggested in a painting through light and shadow by means of a

well-ordered contrast : the most forcible of all oppositions being obtained when the brightest light in a
painting is brought into contact with the most intense
passage of darkness.

Yet this forcible contrast must be employed with
caution or it will be destructive of breadth of effect.
Reynolds has pointed out in his eighth Discourse that
this rule of opposing light to shadow, as given by
Leonardo da Vinci, is one of which the absolute
authority should last only during the painter's student-
ship. "If Leonardo," says he, "had lived to see the
superior splendour and effect which has been produced
by the exactly contrary conduct—by joining light to
light and shadow to shadow—though without doubt
he would have admired it, yet . . . probably it would
not be the first rule with which he would have begun
his instruction." Contrast in short is necessary to
effectiveness but, if it be pressed to the exclusion of
breadth, it will be unpleasant.

The principal figure in a painting, the chief centre
of interest, may be easily accentuated by the use of a
strong contrast of light and darkness, but the device
must be employed with caution. If used without
forethought the result will be too obvious, and will
seem theatrical, as it does in the case of some of
Rembrandt's pupils, or in the popular drawings of
Gustave Doré.

Clever men like Prout often make the mistake of

concentrating the highest light and deepest dark on little figures inserted to give relief and balance, with the result that the eye is attracted to these conventional mannikins, and the effect of the chief masses is over-looked.   On the other hand, if the contrast is concealed or modified by too many flashes of light or spaces of darkness in other parts of the picture, the total effect is apt to be spotty and confused.

Safety lies between these two extremes.   In portraiture we may notice how Titian, Van Dyck and Velasquez repeat the contrast of light and shadow on their sitters' heads, by one or two subordinate contrasts of light on the hands or on some accessory.   The great Dutch painters of genre show similar skill, admitting perhaps two or three minor contrasts to the principal one; whereas our modern realists are in the habit of leaving these things to chance, and have usually far more spots and dots of light and dark in their painting than is conducive to harmonious effect, though the result may gain thereby a certain look of vivacity.

A certain proportion and order must, in fact, be employed in the use of contrast, or the painter may defeat his own ends.   In a small portrait the flash of light in the eyes may be enough to convey the sense of life : in a large painting the machinery must be more complicated.   As diagonal lines convey the feeling of life and motion, so a diagonal disposition of contrast tends to produce the same effect with light and darkness. The arrangement of the squares of a chess-board erected on one of its sides, may thus be taken as a type of the arrangement of light and shade in a picture where an effect of vitality is desired.

By keeping this alternation constantly in mind we obtain also a balance of parts which we can get in no other way If we can imagine a picture as divided into a number of vertical sections by lines extending from the top to the bottom, a good general rule is to ensure that none of these sections shall consist entirely of unbroken light or unbroken darkness.

III

Although the suggestion of infinity in a picture may be aided and emphasised in many different ways, it is, perhaps, most readily produced by means of light and shade. When shadows are filled with vague reflected lights, or when the lights themselves are varied and clouded with faint shadows, the objects in a picture do not proclaim themselves at once, but leave room for the play of the imagination in filling up the parts that are obscured.

The secret of Rembrandt's art is often supposed to lie in the subtlety with which the masses of light and darkness are arranged in his work ; a supposition which has ruined most of his followers and imitators. Some absurd examples will be found in Burnet's book

The real secret lies not so much in the arrangement of the masses as in their quality. In Rembrandt's early works shadows are indeed used to suggest and emphasise form, to give prominence to a figure or a feature, to make things look solid, round and real, or to define their place in the picture scheme. But with experience he found that he could rely upon his drawing to give all the solidity he needed, that the excessive use of shadow as a means of relief made his compositions look artificial or spotty, and that a better effect was produced when shadow was used broadly, as a means of suggesting the vibration and subtlety of atmospheric tone, and for rendering those delicacies of modelling on which all refined and profound expression depends. So in all Rembrandt's mature work shadow is used as a veil, softening outlines which would otherwise have looked harsh, suggesting the play of nature s light upon illumined surfaces, and the mystery of nature's darkness where the illumination was faint.

Mutatis mutandis the method is the same as that employed by a great sculptor, who fills his work with passages of modelling so tender that we seem to feel them rather than to see them, the same as that employed by Leonardo when depicting one of his mysteriously smiling faces, by Gainsborough when building up a world of romance with an apparently careless brush, or by Turner creating a world of palpitating sunlight in which all material things are half revealed and half hidden. To most painters the full charm of this use of shadow is revealed only by long experience. Rembrandt, Gainsborough, and Turner were all hard and precise workers in their youth; so too was Titian. It is only in extreme old age that he paints such things as the Madrid *Entombment* and the Venice *Pietà*.

Nevertheless, even in Titian's early work, we find a deliberate attempt to escape both from the hardness that comes with a too sharp definition of lights and shadows, and impairs the work of such artists as Poussin, and also from the spottiness which comes from using dark shadows as a means of relief, which impairs the work of Tintoret and ruins that of the Bolognese. Titian has not yet conceived of light and shade as a delicate veil of varied tone over the whole picture surface, but he has recognised that if a light or shadow must have a sharp and cutting edge where definition is urgently needed, it must invariably merge softly into the ground elsewhere.

No light or shadow in fact ever tells as a sharply defined patch in Titian's work except where he requires special emphasis. The lights if examined will always be found to have a delicate half-tone at one edge, which connects them with the tone adjoining them: the shadows at some point or other will merge imperceptibly into a lighter tone. The play of sharp edge and soft gradation thus produced, in itself conveys something of the mystery and infinity of the shadow used in Rembrandt's fashion, but not all. Reynolds in most of his portraits inclines to Titian's early method, and his work has thus a slightly more solid and positive quality than that of Gainsborough who, as we have seen, inclines to the looser, more vibrant and more suggestive breadth of Rembrandt.

It is on this ground that we may account for the general superiority of effects in which light masses are relieved from a dark ground, to those in which dark masses are relieved from a light one. In nature these last are often exceedingly powerful, as when objects are seen silhouetted against a bright evening sky: when such effects are rendered in paint they usually look cheap and superficial. The reason seems to lie in the fact that the dark masses do not afford much scope for play of light and shadow, and also separate too obviously and uniformly from the light masses.

By keeping the darker masses comparatively light in tone, as Turner did, and by fusing them where possible with the sky behind, these difficulties may be much reduced. The vigour of the original contrast will be sacrificed, but the gain in unity and subtlety of effect will more than counterbalance the loss. With light masses seen against a dark background such a sacrifice is unnecessary, and the later works of Rembrandt show what force and what infinite variety may be thus produced.

IV

To obtain an effect of repose by the help of light and shade, it is necessary to reverse the devices used to produce vitality. Abrupt contrasts of light and darkness will either be avoided altogether, as was the practice of Whistler in some of his nocturnes and in portraits such as the *Sarasate;* or be modified and softened by ensuring that the large masses of light do not cut sharply against large masses of shadow, but are blended with them by an interposed middle tint, as was the practice of Gainsborough in his most perfect landscapes, and of Crome in such works as the *Mousehold Heath.* There the light upper sky fuses with slightly darker clouds, the clouds in their turn fuse with a still darker distance, and that tone in turn deepens, with the deepening shadow of the great rounded down, into the still darker masses of the foreground.

Even where abrupt contrasts do occur, their effect will be reduced if the contrasting masses are small in proportion to the scale of the picture, and if the general tone be a middle tint with which both darks and lights combine readily. Turner's drawings in general afford countless examples of this last method, as do the paintings of the great artists of China and Japan of the former. The mounting of drawings and the framing of pictures could often be much improved, from the decorative point of view, if this principle were more completely understood.

The size of the picture too is an important factor in the treatment of light and shade. In a miniature, or a very small painting or engraving, the strongest contrasts of dark and light do not oppress the eye. Enlarge them to the size of a mural painting and the result would be intolerable. In fact as the size of a work increases the more careful must we be to see that allowance is made for the quality of repose. Those who decorate buildings will be wise to adopt a scale of tones as limited as that used by Puvis de Chavannes; while the miniature painter may pass abruptly from pure white to intense black without giving offence.

CHAPTER X

EMPHASIS OF COLOUR *

EXPERIENCE seems to indicate that few or no painters who were not good colourists will stand the test of time. Yet most painters are content to leave the question of colour to chance, or at least to employ it without recognising the relation it should bear to the ideas they wish to express. In reality, the sentiment of a picture is emphasised as definitely by the colours in which it is painted as by its design. No picture can produce its complete effect unless its colour be in exact harmony with the emotional mood in which it is conceived.

* An apology is due for the retention of the popular but, I believe, unscientific classification here adopted. My original notes were set down on the lines on which I had grown accustomed to think, and to try to recast them, except at more leisure than I can at present find, would only have led to confusion As a matter of fact, the main conclusions arrived at are independent of chromatic classification, so that the reader will not be seriously misguided For want of sufficient acquaintance I am unable to discuss the system of Prof. Denman W. Ross, of Cambridge, U.S.A. His book, " A Theory of Pure Design " (Boston: Houghton, Mifflin and Co., 1907), is the most elaborate study of rhythm in colour and in pattern which has hitherto appeared

If executed in the sombre tones of Rembrandt, the most sprightly panel by Fragonard would lose all its gaiety: Turner's *Calais Pier* would cease to be menacing if painted with the palette of the *Ulysses and Polyphemus*. Would Titian's superb *Pietà* in the Venice Academy move us so profoundly if it were fired with the radiant glow of the *Bacchus and Ariadne ;* or Piero della Francesca's *Baptism*, if its colour had the gentle beauty of Perugino's triptych on the opposite wall?　It is fantastic to think so.

Yet painters of to-day seem, with but few exceptions, to be blind to this primary condition of their art.　How few landscape painters, for example, in dealing with peaceful country scenery, recognise that the clashing of red tiled roofs, green grass or trees, and bright blue sky is so violent as to destroy at once the effect of repose and harmony they are trying to secure?　A sepia sketch by Claude or Rembrandt conveys a feeling of quiet and serenity, and this will be retained by a good copy in monochrome.　But let us assume the copyist to go a step further and, with the mistaken idea of "finishing" his picture, to paint the grass green, the sky blue and the houses red. The serenity of the original will be lost at once.

As we are not attempting a scientific analysis, we may work on the common and convenient, though unscientific assumption that red, yellow, and blue are the three primary colours.

Of these red is generally admitted to be the most irritating in its effect. A spot of red is thus often used to enliven a picture, but red is seldom made the dominant hue in any but small works of art. Watts, it will be noticed, has used it lavishly in the *Mammon* where his wish was to emphasise cruelty.

Yellow is a fresh exhilarating colour when approximately pure as in the daffodil, the primrose, or in the effects of evening sunlight. Hence comes much of the pleasure we derive from Turner's mature work.

Blue, again, is a fresh and tranquil colour. This character is most apparent in blues such as Prussian or turquoise blue, that are of a slightly greenish tinge. Quite pure blue is somewhat hard, while blues which (like French ultramarine) have the least tinge of red, tend to assume that colour's irritating qualities.

The so-called secondary colours must next be considered.

The effect of purple is difficult to define. When rich and deep it is a noble colour; when paler, as in mauve or lilac, it has the property of catching the eye strongly; but whether pale or deep it is a dangerous colour for the painter to use in any quantity, unless it is subdued in hue, and foiled with green or brown. It is thus employed with fine effect by the Pre-raphaelites. The moment, however, a picture in the least approximates to purple in its general tone, its colour will lmost certainly be bad.

Orange, again, from the nature of its constituents, red and yellow, can rarely be used in any considerable mass without the risk of violence. Even Turner, who was fond of orange, cannot always prevent it from making his work look garish, and by the great Venetians it is never used except in moderation, and in connection with quieter colours such as green and brown.

Green, the remaining secondary colour, is more tractable. When nearly pure, and used in large masses, it may be as strident in effect as any other bright colour; but clear greens, modified only by the very slightest tinge of brown, are often used by the early Flemish masters without unpleasantness, and even when still sharper in tone, as it is found in Millais's *Ophelia* and other Pre-raphaelite pictures, its effect may be no more than stimulating and refreshing. Dark green, however, is a heavy colour that needs very careful management, and light green may look sickly unless foiled with some warmer or darker tone.

The water-colour sketches of De Wint afford many examples of his skill in the use of dark greens, but even that skill does not always preserve him from heaviness in his finished work. The dreadful results produced by amateurs when they paint ivied buildings are sufficient proof of the difficulty De Wint had to face. Admirable examples of the use of light green will be found in Japanese colour-prints; those by Harunobu deserving special notice.

The three tertiaries, brown, gray, and olive, remain to be considered, and their effects are naturally somewhat akin to those of the primary colours that predominate in their respective compositions.

In brown, for example, we meet with red deprived of its irritant hotness by admixture with yellow and blue. It is thus warm and cheerful in effect, and for that reason it is frequently employed as a vehicle for monochrome work, and has been the usual foundation of all elaborate oil-painting up to the middle of the nineteenth century.

In gray, blue is the predominant primary. The result is restful and cool, but may tend to coldness, if the scale be large and the blue tone pronounced. It has been frequently used for monochrome work, especially in landscape, from the readiness with which it suggests the general tone of the air. Its effect is more austere than that of brown, and it is therefore particularly well suited to the representation of grave and serious subjects.

Olive, the remaining tertiary, is always a pleasant colour when used as a foil to stronger colours, but it is rarely used for monochrome, perhaps because, when so employed, it seems akin to green, and therefore raises unnatural associations in the mind if used to represent such things as the sky or the human face.

H

We now come to black and white, which, if not true colours, are at least of the greatest use to the colourist, since besides acting as foils to all other colours they have very definite properties of their own.

Black, by suggesting gloom and darkness, introduces a note of solemnity into any scheme of which it plays a considerable part. It has thus been a favourite with all the great portrait painters Its tone is rapidly modified by the atmosphere so that in landscape it is generally represented by gray. The omission of black from the palette of many modern painters (some of the great Impressionists among them) is perhaps responsible for the lack of grave and serious feeling which characterises their work as a whole, and may explain in part why most modern landscapes look their best in a photographic reproduction.

The effect of pure white in a picture is not the exact reverse of the effect of black. It does not bring cheerfulness and luminosity into a colour-scheme, but conveys no sensation to the mind except that of cold immaculate purity. When it is used in any quantity, the coldness makes itself so strongly felt that the practice of all the great colourists has been to use pure white with the utmost parsimony. Instead they use very pale tones of colour, reserving pure white just for the points of supreme brightness. An examination of such a picture as Titian's *Bacchus and Ariadne* will explain this practice better than any verbal discussion

From this brief analysis it will be seen at once that the general colour of a work of art decides what its sentiment is to be. The glowing russet and blue of Titian, the sombre browns and grays of Rembrandt, the gay tones of Rubens and Watteau, fix the temper of their subjects by the mere first impression they make upon the eye, long before we have time to distinguish what the particular objects represented may be.

All pictures then should have a dominant general colour-scheme in keeping with the sentiment they are intended to convey, and the various devices of the colourist must be exercised within the limits which that sentiment imposes.

I

Our first inquiry must be how best to ensure that our colours will combine into a single united scheme : so that the effect of a picture is that of a harmonious whole, and not of a mere chance aggregate of conflicting hues.

The remarks of Reynolds on this subject seem to point the way more definitely than any theory put forward by scientific writers on the subject. These writers have never, I think, attained much distinction as artists, and, as a rule, their diagrams of harmonious colour refute by their unpleasantness the theories they are intended to illustrate. The truth is that, if any scientific principle of harmony and contrast of colour could be effectively stated, it would be of just so much service to the painter as a perfect theory of human proportion. It would serve as a mean or standard, from which the artist would constantly deviate in search of the emphasis proper to his subject; but a picture painted in exact accord with such a standard would have no more character than a picture built up wholly of figures conforming perfectly to some rigid canon of the ideal human form. What the artist really needs is some precept bearing directly on studio practice, which preserves harmony and yet admits of modification for purposes of emphasis.

Reynolds enunciates the principle that the shadows of a picture should be of the same colour, and thereby form a connecting link between the hues of the lights and the half-lights. The recipe is serviceable, but is somewhat limited in its application. It is naturally most effective when a large portion of a picture consists of shadow, as was usually the case with Reynolds himself, and with artists like Rembrandt. In light pictures it is less serviceable. There the shadows are apt to be too limited in extent, if not too faint as well, to have much binding power and the result may not be satisfactory, unless the various colours are united by some other bond.

Another principle of Reynolds that the whites in a picture, and indeed the high lights in general, should be of a warm tinge, "as if illuminated by the setting sun," though valuable as a protection against the more harsh and chilly forms of bad colour, is also too limited in range to be of much practical service in producing fine colour consistently.   The use of a brown varnish to "tone" cold or garish oil paintings has long been recognised: brightly coloured Japanese prints on the same principle are sometimes stained with coffee to make them more saleable, and many "Old Masters" are undoubtedly rendered more harmonious in effect by the mellowing influence of time and dirt.

Much, however, of the finest colour in which we take pleasure is distinctly cool in quality and cannot be referred to this principle: nor can we always or often recognise the employment of the somewhat similar precept, attributed by tradition to Rubens, that colours should be arranged in definite sequence, beginning with white at the source of light, followed in turn by yellow, orange, red, and blue.

A criticism by Reynolds, on a picture submitted to him by a young marine painter, contains the germ of a more vital truth.   He observed that the picture lacked harmony because it was painted with too great a variety of colours, adding that a picture should look as if it was all painted from the same palette.

There can be no doubt I think that Sir Joshua intended to convey, by this remark, the idea that safety lay in employing only one definite set of pigments on each picture. His own practice and that of Gains-borough certainly show that both these great colourists worked on some such principle. Both were masters of a considerable variety of methods and pigments, but they did not use them all together on a single canvas. For each new picture they employed just the few pigments sufficient to carry out the work in hand, and no more. Black and white, with one red, one yellow, one blue, and one brown make the palette from which their most splendid harmonies are drawn. In modern times the theory has been most emphatically restated by Whistler, without however receiving one tithe of the attention which it merited.

If we turn to the sister art of ceramics, in which the most glowing and daring harmonies of colour known to us have been attained, we find that in Damascus ware and in Chinese porcelain the most splendid effects are produced with a similar limited palette. Nevertheless the limitation is not the whole secret, for many modern coloured wares employ a small number of pigments, and yet are unpleasing to the eye. To find what these further conditions are, it may be well to take some form of art in which the growth, development and decline of the colour sense can be more or less definitely traced, as in the case of Japanese colour-prints.

Here a survey of the field shows that iteration of a few selected tints is a constant factor in success

When the tints are very few, as in the early part of the eighteenth century, the results are charming but perhaps rather monotonous. When the number and subtlety of the tints is increased by Harunobu, Kiyonaga, and Utamaro, the process is perfected. When, at the end of the century, the Japanese artist was introduced to garish aniline colours, the effect has still a certain coherency, even though the individual tones are violent. The rigid iteration, which is a necessity of this Japanese method, still makes for unity even when the components are discordant, but complete success is attained only when the iteration is combined with fine quality of individual tints.

How then does a pleasing tint differ from an unpleasing one? Is it not that it is never quite flat or quite positive? Is it not in itself a little picture, in which two or more sets of colour atoms lie together side by side, and by their iterations produce that very effect of harmonious variety which the masses of pigment in a picture produce upon a larger scale? In any book of coloured papers the broken tints, such as those which pass under the name of granite, are invariably pleasanter to the eye than primary colours, or than tints immediately derived from them.

Any colour, too, that is printed on a very smooth or shiny paper will be less pleasant than one printed on a "matt" or grained surface, simply because the irregularities of the surface in the latter case cast shadows, and bring a second and darker tone to play side by side with that originally printed. On a smooth paper the original tone has to depend entirely upon itself; no secondary tint is formed by shadows, and the effect will tend to be flat and lifeless. The difference can be well studied by comparing a good colour-print on soft fibrous Japanese paper with the most elaborate reproduction of one by lithography on smooth European paper. However carefully the individual tints have been matched, the difference in quality of hue is incalculable.

Having then good reason for suspecting that colour harmony depends upon the iteration of tints which themselves have a certain internal iteration or vibrancy, let us test our hypothesis upon the works of European artists.

Taking first the works of the primitive Flemings, of whom the Van Eycks and Memling are typical examples, we can see at once how their method of transparent painting over a white ground gives all their individual colours a degree of vibrancy, a gem-like brilliancy, which was never quite equalled by subsequent painters.

Thus even in their portraits, where deliberate repetition of tones was less possible than in a subject piece, the mere quality of the pigment is enough to convey a sense of harmonious colour. When we come to the work of a later master, Rubens, the colours are rather less perfectly transparent, but they are interchanged and repeated with much more science, so that the colour harmony is no less complete than in the earlier work, although it is pitched in a different key.

It would be easy to quote similar examples from among the great Venetians, who rightly hold the first place as colourists among the various schools of Italy. It will however be enough to refer to the lavish use they make of patterned stuffs, in which repetition of colours is ever present, and to the peculiar glow and vibration of their pigments, the secret of which (probably depending upon the use of a tempera ground under the oil painting) has long been lost.

To come to our own time, it will be noticed that the colour of the great Impressionists such as Monet, Sisley, and Degas, though exceedingly bright and daring, has also a certain unity of its own, due not only to the talent of the artists, but to the fact that all the individual tones are built up of interlaced patches of the primary colours. Repetition of these colours is necessarily carried through the whole picture.

This repetition, of course, is characteristic of the colouring of outdoor nature. The shadows over a distant landscape reflect the colour of the sky and clouds above them; sometimes so completely that the local colour is practically absorbed. When the sky is blue, and the clouds light and scattered, a cloud shadow often looks bright blue; if the clouds are numerous and purple, the very same piece of country will assume their purple hue, solely from the influence of the light reflected from above, while in the foreground the upper surface of every leaf and blade of grass is tinged with the colour of the sky. A great part of the work of the Impressionists has been the study and emphatic statement of these reflections, and the public suspicion of their work would have been overcome long ago, had the truths they enunciate been expressed with less disdain for recognised pictorial quality.

It is sometimes urged that, if colours are fine and vibrant in themselves, their arrangement does not matter. Such colours certainly may not be unpleasant in effect even if they are not deliberately repeated, but there can be no doubt that their power is immensely enhanced through the emphasis secured by intelligent repetition. The colour-prints of the minor Japanese are for this reason scattered and aimless in effect when compared with those of Harunobu, Kiyonaga, or Utamaro, just as the paintings of a Bonifazio are inferior to those of a Titian.

II

The sensation of vitality may evidently be imparted by the use of bright colours alone, as in the case of advertisement posters, but for the more domestic process of oil painting this simple method is often unsuitable. Conditions of subject-matter and decorative function usually demand a large proportion of quiet tones, and the introduction of life and vigour into these tones may be a matter of some difficulty.

The use of colours of a warm tint, *i.e.*, with a preponderance of red and yellow, will do something towards this end. But there can be no doubt that the real way of introducing vitality into colour is by devising a colour contrast of a suitable kind, and the sharper the contrast, the more lively will be the sensation produced in the mind of the spectator. If the contrast be between two shades of blue, as in some of the nocturnes of Whistler, the sense of vitality conveyed will not be strong, because the two tones differ so little, and because blue is naturally a quiet colour. Were one of these nocturnes translated into a Turnerian scheme of delicate red and yellow, the sense of vitality would be stronger ; were the contrast one of bright blue and bright red, it would be so strong as to rob the work altogether of its tranquillity.

It is for this reason that a coat of cool colour will possess more vitality, when laid over a warm colour, than if laid over another cool tint similar to itself in hue and tone. In the former case, wherever the ground shows through, the vibration of the two opposing tints will be lively. In the latter case the upper and lower tints will be so alike that there will be little or no vibration, and the effect will be dead. Hence the danger of repainting any part of a picture, without ensuring that the new paint is laid over a ground which differs from it considerably in colour.

Again, where the contrast is carried forcibly through a picture, as in Titian's *Bacchus and Ariadne*, where strong blue and russet, or strong blue and scarlet, are everywhere opposed, the effect is more stirring than in his *Noli me tangere*, where the quiet blue of the sky is separated from the quieter crimson of the Magdalen's dress by a large mass of neutral browns and greens. As Reynolds pointed out long ago, the style of painting in which strong colours are sharply opposed to one another in large masses, is more grand and striking than one where the colours are used with but moderate force and are tenderly blended.

Also, the place in a picture where the contrast of colour is strongest will inevitably tend to attract the eye. It should therefore correspond with the focus of interest, lest the spectator's attention be diverted. The device, commonly employed by a previous generation of landscape painters, of introducing a figure in a scarlet cloak to enliven by contrast a scheme of cool blues and greens, was open to objection on this score. The eye was inevitably drawn to the bright red spot, and finding there only a conventional little figure, was disappointed and confused.

If a painter finds himself face to face with the same difficulty, and sees his picture suffering from

inertness of colour, he would be wise, I think, to consider carefully where the focus of interest lies, and try
to heighten the colour contrasts in its immediate neigh-
bourhood before attempting to introduce or emphasise
any accessories, strengthening cool colours if the general
tone be warm, and warm ones if the general tone be
cool.

Lastly, since harmony depends on repetition, a
picture will consist of a series of colour contrasts most
forcible at or near the focus of interest, and less forcible in the subordinate parts. Into this ordered
scheme a contrast of the most striking kind can be
introduced by the employment of some different colour,
found nowhere else in the picture, and made doubly
emphatic by its isolation. It is, however, a device
rather for emergencies than for general use since, if
the isolated colour is used in any considerable mass, it
may disturb the harmony of the whole scheme.

Vitality of general effect is, however, most readily
produced when the colours composing a picture are
separated by definite contours. This system is found
in all the early European schools up to the time of
Titian, in the colour-prints of Japan, in the porcelain
of China, and in the faience of Persia and the nearer
East. If we compare these various schools of fine
colour with the colour produced by later masters
such as Gainsborough or Delacroix, we shall notice
that the work of the former group is more cheerful

than that of the latter, as well as more brilliant. It
conveys the impression of a younger, simpler, and
perhaps a happier world ; while the painters whose
tones melt imperceptibly into each other seem perhaps
more sensitive, but are certainly more pensive or more
sombre. Colour contrasts, in fact, like tone contrasts,
can be made much more lively and forcible if the
contours of the constituent masses are kept sharp and
definite, as in a patchwork quilt, a map, or a stained
glass window.

III

No less important than vitality of colour is subtlety
of colour. Good colour is never a positive thing of
which every part can be definitely described, but the
tints are so constantly gradated and interchanged that
no two square inches, even of a large picture, will be
exactly alike. In good pictures, even the colours which
appear to be unbroken reds and blues resolve themselves, when seen closely, into complex tints of infinite
variety.

Great colourists appear to obtain the infinite play of
hue without effort, and it is only when we see their
early works, that we find traces of the labour by which
they acquired their mastery. Nor does a survey of
the field of painting show any one royal road to this
power of producing subtle colour. With the early

masters of Italy it is produced by the delicate interweaving of tempera brush strokes: with Titian and the
Venetians it seems to depend upon the laying of a film
of semi-opaque oil paint over a luminous ground: with
the Flemings in general it is produced by transparent
or translucent painting over a thin brown preparation.
Turner often worked in very thin colour on a ground of
solid white; Watts used successive scumbles of
pigment so stiff as to be nearly dry. The Pre-
Raphaelites and the Impressionists alike depended on
minute touches of pure, bright colours; Gainsborough
worked with large loose sweeps of secondary and
tertiary hues. Every colourist in fact, however much
he may have learned from his predecessors, has always
had to work out his own salvation in the end, by
finding for himself the method which best expresses
his personal ideals.

The difficulty of the matter lies in the fact that
success and failure in colour lie within such narrow
limits. A careful copy may from some slight additional
heaviness of handling, imperceptible except to a trained
eye, lose all the colour-quality of the original from
which it is taken. Even when the tints seem perfectly
matched, a slight difference in surface will alter the
effect. A shiny paper, for example, may go far to
destroy the subtlety of any tone printed upon it, while
a coat of varnish may transform a dull expanse of paint
into a masterpiece.

The constant study of fine colour both in painting and in other forms of art, such as Chinese porcelain and Persian faience, may do something towards the education of a colourist; the knowledge that constant gradation or vibration lies at the root of the whole matter may do a little; but the faculty of appreciating subtle colour depends, or seems to depend, upon a fineness of perception in things not mathematically demonstrable, and upon a boldness of invention which must in some degree be inborn.

Certain methods, however, may be recommended to the beginner by which his first steps may be rendered comparatively painless. If we work in oil, the use of a transparent brown underpainting, in the manner of Rubens, allows more positive colours to be introduced gradually, and enables those whose progress is difficult to go work which, if not inventive, is at least not actively unpleasant to the eye.

Perhaps the greatest trouble of all in connection with colour is the fact that its most subtle qualities are often revealed by accident, and seem to be dependent on a certain degree of incompletion. A sketch is almost always more pleasant in colour than a highly finished picture. The more, indeed, we re-work our pigments the less will be their purity and vibrant quality. If we wish to alter them, we must do so in the way Reynolds recommends, by laying on more colour, not by messing about that which we have already got.

Freshness and directness in fact are akin to quality and subtlety.

One other property of subtle colour remains to be noticed. It is rarely or never associated with strong relief. All the best colourists, from the time of the primitives to our own day, avoid excess of roundness in their modelling. Their masses approach as nearly to flatness as is compatible with significance, and perhaps the finest schools of colouring in the world are those of China and Japan from which relief is wholly abolished. If we examine carefully a fine example of Titian or Gainsborough or Turner we shall be struck by the very low scale of relief which is employed. The sense of solidity always seems to be obtained with the smallest possible range of tone. Even painters like Reynolds, whose contrast of tones is forcible and who admit dark shadows, always take care that their lights shall incline to flatness, and shall be delicately modelled inside that apparent flatness. In this respect it will be seen that the use of colour is apparently governed by a similar principle to that which holds good with light and shade, namely that rounded modelling is inimical, if not invariably fatal, to complete success.

IV

From what has already been said about colour, it is not difficult to see how restfulness of colour may be attained.

I

The most obvious way of all is to use secondary and tertiary tones, especially those in which blue rather than yellow or red is the dominant quality. Iteration, as we have seen, will do much to secure unity, but the unity so produced may not be pleasant to the eye. A poster, for example, some ten feet square may have a certain unity, though executed in glaring red and purple, if the constituent colours are sufficiently interwoven and repeated. Yet its total effect on the eye will none the less be unpleasant, from the sheer impact of the violent colours of which it is composed. But this same scheme of colour, were it reduced to the scale of a miniature in an illuminated manuscript, might look no more than pleasantly bright.

Harmony, in fact, is limited by the power of the eye to endure the shock of strong colour without pain. A miniature may be painted in vivid colours: the same colours used on a large scale would be overwhelming.

When using primary or secondary colours on the scale of a fair-sized easel picture, we must not only repeat them, but must separate them as far as possible from each other. We may modify them further by the addition of a certain proportion of tertiary colour, and this proportion must be increased with the scale of the picture. Red, or colours like violet and orange which contain red, must be managed with special caution, for the irritating element in them is strong enough to overwhelm a proportion of neutral tints sufficient to make blue and yellow harmonious.

The choice of a tertiary to modify a contrast between two strong colours will naturally be determined by the particular emphasis desired. For example, in a landscape, red walls or roofs may make a sharp contrast with green grass or trees. Supposing we wished to modify that contrast, which would be the best tertiary to employ? The answer depends upon the part of the subject which we wish to emphasise most. If the green trees are the subject, then we shall accentuate their greenness by working on a brown ground, which will serve as a contrast to them and will soften the force of the reds. On the other hand, if the buildings were the principal thing, a gray tone would blend with the greens and make the reds stand out sharply. In the same way if some colour in a picture seems unduly obtrusive, yet alteration be undesirable, its effect may be moderated by the introduction, in some other part of the picture, of a still stronger and larger mass of similar colour.

The second way of securing repose in colour is by doing away, so far as possible, with sharp edges so that the tones melt imperceptibly into one another. The process, however, is a dangerous one as it entices many artists into a feeble and woolly method of work. It should not be forgotten that the last manner of Corot and Turner who carried the process as far as it can be carried safely, was founded on years of practice in a singularly dry and precise style. For the beginner, at least, the intelligent use of tertiary colours to modify strong contrasts is a safer principle than the blurring of contours. This blurring too often results in ruining the stability of the design, and without stable design we can produce nothing except trifles.

Lastly, if we find that a design promises to be too turbulent, we can make it restful by reducing the pitch of the colouring throughout: if necessary, till it is little more than monochrome. The landscapes of Gainsborough owe much of their charm to the consummate skill with which he reduces the sharp blues of nature to delicate gray or turquoise, and her sharp greens to broken tones of olive and golden brown. The works of Rembrandt and Hals or, among more modern artists, of Daumier and Millet, frequently exhibit the same practice. Nature's scheme of bright sharp hues is transposed into one of grave majestic tones, and these convey a spirit of solemnity which would be entirely dissipated by more lively colouring. If one of Millet's sombre peasant groups were surrounded by the vivid greens and blues of a Constable sketch, it would instantly lose its impressiveness.

In practice this reduction is often far from an easy matter. Every colour in a picture is affected by its neighbours, so that if we wish to lower the pitch of some too prominent colour, we must lower all the rest in exact proportion. Many of the most delightful effects of colour depend on such reductions. Turner, for example, makes brown look like red, and gray look like blue, by contrasting them skilfully with their complementary tones. When the reduction of pitch is small the eye will overlook minor inequalities; when it is very great the result approaches monochrome and once more becomes manageable. It is the intermediate stage which is difficult, but as it is also the most fascinating it is well worth all the study we can devote to it. Special prominence was given to Gainsborough in the preceding paragraph because, among comparatively modern masters, he is the one who has perhaps succeeded best in holding an exact balance between excessive brightness and complete renunciation of positive colour, both in landscape and portraiture. In comparison with him, Constable would seem crude; and, at the other end of the scale, Millet would seem limited.

In making this reduction one factor must always be kept in mind. As the reduction approaches monochrome, the emphasis of our colour weakens and emphasis of light and shade takes its place. Our new scheme of transposed colour must thus be adjusted to correspond with that emphasis, and possibly must sacrifice some accent of its own to do so.

A neglect of this condition causes many pictures, notably those by the minor masters of the Dutch

School, to look better in photography than in their original paint.   They are designed in light and shade, but the emphasis of the touches of colour is not identical with that of the fundamental design, and the result, in spite of the individual tones being quiet, is confused and unrestful.   In certain English water-colour drawings we may notice the same fault.   For example, we find architecture cleverly drawn in quiet tones of brown and orange, but the addition of a blue sky destroys all this repose by competing with the build-ings, and distracting the spectator's eye from what really should be the principal subject.   A wash of gray would have given the effect of atmosphere equally well, and by its subordination to the buildings would have left them their predominance.

PART II

EMPHASIS OF MATERIALS

"Sumite materiam vestris qui pingitis æquam
Viribus."
                                    After the ARS POETICA.

CHAPTER XI

PROCESSES OF DRAWING

THE materials at the artist's disposal are so various, and differ so widely in their nature, application and functions, that any attempt to analyse them as a whole on the method hitherto followed would be more complicated than practical. It will therefore be most satisfactory to deal with the chief artistic processes one by one. These processes may for convenience be grouped under three heads:

    1. Processes of Drawing.

    2. Processes of Engraving.

    3. Processes of Painting.

We may at once turn to the consideration of the first group, that of Processes of Drawing. These processes may be regarded as being five in number.

    1. Silverpoint Drawing.

    2. Pen Drawing.

    3. Drawing with pencil or hard chalk.

    4. Drawing with pastel or charcoal.

    5. Brush Drawing.

SILVERPOINT DRAWING

The process of drawing with a gold or silver wire upon a sheet of paper washed with zinc white has been a favourite one with great masters. The pale gray line produced by the touch of the metal point has a cleanness and crispness resembling that produced by a stroke of the graver, while the possibility of working on a slightly tinted ground often makes the result a thing of singular beauty. Unity is secured by the correspondence between the pale tone of the work and the paper on which it is executed. This paleness of tone is a disadvantage when the quality aimed at is vitality; then the bolder contrasts of black chalk, or the emphatic strokes and angles of drawings made with the pen or point of the brush, would be more fitting.

In subjects, however, where infinite gradation of touch, statement of delicate detail, and subtle purity of tone are needed, as in drawings of women and children and indeed in portraiture generally, silverpoint is invaluable. Considering the example set by Raphael and Leonardo it is curious that silverpoint should not be in more general use among our portrait draughtsmen, for it is restful as well as delicate. Possibly the worship of what is obviously vigorous has for the time being blunted our perceptive sense, and has led to this undeserved neglect. A few exquisite landscape drawings too have been made in silverpoint, but its possibilities in this field have not yet been really explored and might repay exploration well.

PEN DRAWING

Drawing with the quill or reed pen was generally practised by the old masters, both in studies from the model and in sketches for compositions. The pen was usually charged with bistre, or some other neutral brown pigment. The drawings thus were pleasant in aspect, while the cleanness and precision of the touch introduced a force and spirit which no other medium could surpass. Only a very small degree of gradation is obtainable in a pen stroke, and the great masters, when they needed gradation, generally obtained it by reinforcing their pen drawings with washes of colour applied with the brush.

The drawings of Rembrandt exhibit the flexibility of this method to perfection; indeed, in his hands pen drawing assumes a force and subtlety which others have hardly succeeded in equalling by lengthy processes of painting. The effect of drawings like those of Campagnola, where gradation of tone is sought by making the line work elaborate, are much inferior in effect to those where the decisive pen lines are reinforced with the brush. The perfecting of the steel pen enabled the Pre-raphaelites to execute some marvellous drawings with the finish of miniatures: then, with the rise of process-engraving, pen drawing changed its character. The photographic process demanded neat, open decisive work, in clear regular strokes, without blotting or washing or very fine lines, executed in very black ink upon very white paper or cardboard.

The decorative beauty of the older drawings was thus sacrificed almost universally, as a comparison of a drawing by Charles Keene with a piece of good modern work will prove. Inartistic conditions indeed have not prevented some delightful work being done, but, with one or two possible exceptions, the best of it has been done for our humorous papers, where a certain freedom of tradition has survived from the great days of wood engraving and lithography, and where the qualities needed are rather a merry eye and a quick hand, than tender insight or great intellectual power.

DRAWING WITH PENCIL OR HARD CHALK

As silverpoint is the medium for subjects that need extreme refinement of contour, and the pen for subjects that need spirit and sharpness, so the pencil or hard chalk may be regarded as mediums of general utility, being hard enough to give reasonable precision of form, and yet soft enough to give delicate gradations of tone.

The pencil is specially popular from its handiness

and portability, so its advantages over all other mediums in these respects outweigh, for many, its disadvantages. No medium can be used so readily, or can suggest so much with so little trouble and preparation. It is thus invaluable to those who have to depend upon rapid notes, or have to sketch under difficult conditions. The comparative weakness or poverty of the effect it produces, and the shiny surface which graphite is apt to leave, can be avoided or concealed by a skilful draughtsman, but for all elaborate work, especially for such as can be done in a studio, hard chalk gives far better results.

The pen or the silverpoint were preferred to chalk by the artists of the Quattrocento ; possibly because the precise detail which could be obtained with them was akin to the precise detail demanded of the tempera painter. The moment, however, that the use of the oil medium became general, and breadth of effect was preferred to sharp definition, the use of black and red chalk became customary. Raphael and Michelangelo, Holbein and Rubens made their noblest drawings with black or red chalk ; while, later, in the hands of Gainsborough, and above all in those of Watteau, these materials proved not only their fitness for an entirely different order of subject-matter, but also their power of conveying the sense of colour.

The example of Watteau has proved, too, that chalk can be used with a minute precision almost rivalling that of silverpoint; but not one draughtsman in a million could expect to emulate that enchanting virtuoso, and the majority of those who draw in chalk must expect to have to work on a larger scale than the draughtsmen who use a sharp pointed instrument. Subject to this condition, and granting a moderate use of the stump or the brush to produce or to soften flat tones, there is hardly any subject either in figure or landscape work to which hard chalk will not do justice; no medium is at once more spirited and more precise, more forcible and more delicate.

DRAWING WITH PASTEL OR CHARCOAL

⌐ Hard chalk, however, has but little favour in these days compared with pastel and charcoal. Possibly we have lost something of the sense of the vigour and value of line which our forerunners possessed, and do not wish to follow contours so firmly as they: possibly the coming of Impressionism has taught men to look for colour and sunlight, and to let delineation of the forms take care of itself. Whatever the cause, charcoal, soft chalk and pastel are the favourite materials to-day for sketches and studies where oil or water colour cannot be used.

With charcoal and soft chalk we certainly get great richness of shadow, strength of tone, and, by wiping or rubbing out, great brilliancy of light.   These qualities make the medium suitable for landscape, portrait and figure subjects, when dramatic effect is more desirable than subtlety. These dramatic effects, however, come so readily with charcoal that drawings made with it are apt to look showy and superficial.

Pastel has many conveniences for the student of colour. Its softness, however, compels a certain lack of definition, and though this vagueness is serviceable in some classes of landscape work, and to a less extent in portraiture, it is apt to entice the student into the making of endless slight studies, charming perhaps as far as they go, but rarely going as far as a good artist should desire. This defect can be mitigated by working on rather a large scale, but it can never be entirely overcome.

On the other hand pastels, being used dry, do not suffer the loss of luminosity which occurs when a pigment is diluted with any liquid medium. Pastel therefore is naturally adapted for the notation of vivid effects of light and colour, and this power is increased by the fact that, for mixed tints, the component hues can be hatched across each other, and so do not lose brightness as wet pigments do when they are mingled intimately. The texture of such hatched work may not be pleasant, indeed the tone of pastel even when softened by the stump is apt to be startling to eyes accustomed to other pigments, but there are occasions when every atom of colour and light which can be preserved ought to be preserved, and for those occasions pastel is the appropriate medium. When quieter tones have to be rendered, and that is the case with the vast majority of subjects, other mediums give finer results than pastel. Logically perhaps, pastel, admitting as it does the use of a full set of colours, should be included among processes of painting. Yet it has really little in common with these processes, and it seems better to deal with it in connection with drawing in soft chalk, for to that it is, in practice, more nearly akin.

BRUSH DRAWING

Brush drawing on the other hand is akin to painting in the matter of execution, but to drawing proper in its results. In Europe, monochrome drawing with the brush has been almost invariably executed on paper. On that material the brush leaves a sharp impression, well suited to vivid and lively notes, while the flexibility of the point allows great freedom of handling. Yet this very flexibility makes the brush a difficult thing to control, so that brush drawings are comparatively rare things, and are commonly made only by those who are very facile executants. The quality gained by the brush is one of swiftness and spirit, and this quality is apt to vanish when the wash is in the slightest degree disturbed or modified by subsequent retouching. The brush is thus ill-suited for any subject that demands delicacy of tone and modelling, for these can only be obtained by comparatively slow careful manipulation. The early masters sometimes, it is true, obtained these effects by using a very small fine pointed brush in the manner of a pen; but the drawings so made, however delicate, would have looked more crisp and masterly had they been done with silverpoint.

In China and Japan, where the brush has for centuries been used for drawing upon silk as well as paper, the results obtained are remarkable. Being trained from childhood to handle the brush, with the aid of a well-established routine of practice, these Oriental artists acquire a certainty of touch and a flexibility of arm, wrist and fingers such as few Europeans can boast. Swiftness is an essential of the process, so that this flexibility stands them in good stead, while they are further assisted by the pictorial convention of their continent, which renounces the imitation of relief by means of light and shade. The Oriental artist is concerned only with the character of the things he represents. The European is always thinking of imitating the appearance they present to the eye: he is not content, till the bulk, the roundness and the surface modelling of the objects before him are rendered with all the force of light and shade and relief which his materials permit him to use. The sharp touch of the brush is thus as ill-adapted to the

K

elaborate modelling of Europe as it is suitable to the vivid sketching of the Oriental. Unless we deliberately imitate Oriental methods, we shall find that the brush satisfies us better when reinforcing other materials, such as the pen, the pencil or hard chalk, than when used by itself.

The last few years have witnessed in England a remarkable revival of the use of the pen, the pencil and the brush for making studies. The results obtained fully vindicate the superiority of these materials to the pastels, soft chalk and charcoal which were commonly employed by the previous generation of students.

CHAPTER XII

PROCESSES OF ENGRAVING

THE processes of engraving may be most conveniently classified under three headings, according to the materials on which the engraving is made.

     1. Engraving on wood.

     2. Engraving on stone.

     3. Engraving on metal.

ENGRAVING ON WOOD

The principle of all wood engraving is the same. The whites are cut out from the surface of a flat block, leaving the dark portions in relief, to be printed either in a press, as in Europe, or by rubbing, as is the custom in the East. The tool used in the older forms of wood engraving was a sharp pointed knife, and the cutting was done on comparatively soft woods, in the direction of the grain. Up to the beginning of the nineteenth century this was the universal practice in Europe, and still remains so in China and Japan. Both in Europe and the East this cutting became a highly specialised craft, and the common practice was for the artist to make his drawing in line on the wood block and then to hand it over to the engraver to be cut. The magnificent engravings by Lützelberger, after Holbein's designs for his *Dance of Death,* illustrate the perfection of workmanship which was thus attained, even though it was attained at the cost of some of the peculiar characteristics of the medium.

The wood-engraver, in reality, works in white on a black ground, since every incision he makes tells as a light when printed. His method is thus analogous to that of a draughtsman working with body colour on a dark ground. Almost every artist, however, who drew for wood engraving, drew with dark pigment on a light ground. Wood engraving thereby was perverted into an imitation of pen and ink drawing—a perversion which survived and was intensified when the use of the graver was discovered, and the substitution of hard boxwood (cut across the grain) for softer woods (cut in the direction of the grain), allowed the cutting of the most minute and regular lines.

Although in the prints of Bewick and his school, made when the new process was in its infancy, we may note the skilful use made of white lines on a strong black ground, the general tendency set towards a still closer imitation of pen work than had been possible with the knife, which culminated in the wonderful cuts after Millais, Sandys, Houghton and the other English "artists of the sixties." The true tradition survived only in the little prints of William Blake and Edward Calvert, so it is under their influence that the few notable modern exponents of wood engraving have worked. Their achievements prove that wood engraving has powers which have never been sufficiently exploited, and are well worth the attention of those who are in search of a powerful means of dealing with romantic subjects. The reproductive engravings of Mr. Timothy Cole indicate, on the other hand, that wood engraving may, in skilful hands, almost rival mezzotint in delicacy of tone, though his elaborate methods are less likely to be of use to the creative artist than the splendid directness of Blake.

Unity, vitality, and repose are qualities natural to straightforward woodcutting: add to this its potentialities in the matter of colour-printing (of which Japan has provided such splendid examples), and no claim made for it will seem extravagant.

ENGRAVING ON STONE

Lithography, the art of taking impressions from a drawing made on a fine grained stone or prepared paper, with a special kind of greasy chalk, is a comparatively modern invention. It has unfortunately been put to commercial uses even more frequently than wood engraving, and its finest tradition, until the time of

Whistler, is limited to a few works by Goya, and a large number of drawings, mostly for illustrated periodicals, by Daumier, and other Frenchmen of less talent, of whom Guys was perhaps the most striking and Raffet the most popular.

In the hands of Goya and Daumier lithography becomes a medium of great power, although, in Daumier's case, the quality of the prints is not invariably pleasant, as they were produced cheaply to serve the needs of the moment. The pale gray tones obtainable in lithography caught the fancy of Whistler, and he developed the art to a pitch of refinement which no other lithographer has attained, his use of the brush in one or two rare washed lithographs being, I believe, without parallel. His best lithographs are in quality as fine as the best of his etchings, and there can hardly be higher praise than that. Yet the secret was a personal one, for his most accomplished modern follower, Mr. C. H. Shannon, has never attained quite the same delicacy, although he has extended the application of the medium to elaborate effects of shimmering light. The other living artists who have tried lithography have not had so much success.

It remains however a fine medium, either for emphatic statements of tragedy and satire, as with Goya and Daumier, or for artists like Whistler, Fantin Latour and Shannon, who are in love with certain phases of delicate illumination. The ordinary painter will probably find he can work far more easily with common chalk on paper, and get more spirited effects with the etching needle.

ENGRAVING ON METAL

The processes of engraving on metal may roughly be divided into two sections.

I. Processes in which the metal is cut with a tool; as in line engraving, stipple engraving, dry-point, or mezzotint.

II. Processes in which the metal is eaten away by an acid; as in etching and aquatint.

LINE ENGRAVING

Of all these numerous processes, line engraving deserves the first place. A plate of copper or soft steel is cut by a sharp V-shaped tool, which turns up a little ridge of metal on each side of the furrow it makes. These ridges are removed with a scraper, the plate is covered with ink, wiped, and then pressed into a damp sheet of paper to which the ink lines are transferred.

The line thus produced has a character of its own. Considerable strength has to be exerted by the engraver in forcing his tool through the metal. So the pressure has to be evenly applied, to prevent the line being of uneven depth, and carefully controlled, to prevent it from slipping out of the proper course. The process is in consequence slow, and the line produced, though firm in quality, and well adapted to follow a sweeping curve, cannot possess the freedom and flexibility of a line drawn with more tractable materials. The great tradition of line engraving is thus one of austerity. Although certain of the early Florentine engravings have singular grace, and the same quality shows in some of the prints of Schongauer, great masters of the art such as Mantegna and Marcantonio in Italy, Dürer and Lucas van Leyden in Northern Europe, agree in utilising to the full the precise and severe quality of the engraved line.

Later, as with wood engraving, this feeling for character of line was lost in the search for effects of tone, and it is undeniable that, when used for purposes of reproduction, line engraving produced wonderful results, of which the engraved portraits and figure subjects of eighteenth-century France, and the prints after Turner in the nineteenth-century England, represent the culmination. The processes by which these wonderful results were attained were, however, so elaborate that a creative artist could hardly pursue them with advantage, even if the skill of Turner's engravers, which was the outcome of generations of professional experience and apprenticeship and the oversight of a most keen and critical genius, could ever be recovered.

Nor is any general revival of the older tradition of line engraving probable in these days of photogravure, especially since the process can represent such things as trees only by an obvious convention. Yet, when this age of naturalistic experiment is over, the noble quality of the line produced may tempt some considerable artist to apply the medium once more to a loftier order of subjects than the heraldic work to which it is at present restricted. And he may apply it with success, so long as subtlety of contour, and perfection of spacing are made the ideals; while the rendering of tone is kept within the strictest possible bounds, even if it be not altogether discarded. Unity and repose such simple engraving will in some measure possess naturally; infinity must be sought in the subtlety of the contours; vitality will be the one quality which the engraver will find it hardest to supply.

STIPPLE ENGRAVING

The process, once so popular, of engraving by means of dots punched in a metal plate is, like line engraving, of great antiquity, but may be dismissed much more briefly. Though some pretty plates were produced in this manner during the eighteenth century, and the process has often been a useful adjunct to line engraving, it has never been used for original work by any considerable artist. It has the double disadvantage of being laborious in execution as well as weak in effect, and so, although it is not inappropriate to certain trivial subjects, few would care to waste time over it when better results can be got far more readily by other means. Technically I believe the word "stipple" is restricted to work reinforced by biting; where the work is done without acid it is said to be "in the dot manner."

DRY-POINT

Dry-point is a process similar to line engraving in that the lines are cut directly upon a plate of metal with a sharp tool, but different from it in one important respect. In line engraving the effect of the printed line is dependent chiefly upon the ink retained in the V-shaped furrow cut by the graver; in dry-point it is dependent almost entirely upon the ink retained by the rough edges of metal turned up by the passage of the tool through the surface of the plate. The purity of the line produced by engraving depends on the removal of these rough edges, or at least upon their subordination to the furrow cut by the graver. The richness of dry-point depends upon their retention, and the furrow cut by the tool is of small importance. These rough edges retain the printing ink and, under the printer's hands, produce a line of rich and velvety blackness, of a depth and quality unattainable in any other process of engraving. Unfortunately the rough edges of metal on which the effect depends cannot be made to bear the stress of printing ; after the first few proofs are taken, their serrations are broken off or smoothed down, their power of retaining ink is diminished, and each successive proof is perceptibly weaker than its predecessor.

Again, the process of drawing directly upon a metal plate is not easy work, although the substitution, in recent years, of a diamond for a metal point has done much to remove its difficulties. It demands strength in the fingers while, even with strength and experience, it is difficult to make the metal point move freely, and at the same time retain force. It is thus inherently unsuited for the rendering either of precise and subtle contour, or for exact gradations of tone. Dry-point cannot well be used for imitating nature ; it can suggest her forms only by a convention, and her tones only by broad opposition of light and darkness.

A medium which so imperatively calls for selection and concentration can be employed with success only by experienced artists. The record of dry-point is thus remarkable. Used first by Rembrandt as a means of enriching the shadows of his etched plates, it subsequently usurped the place of bitten work in his affections, and his large prints of *The Three Crosses* and *Christ Presented to the People* remain the two supreme monuments to the power of dry-point. With Rembrandt's death it went out of fashion, no doubt because it was unsuited to the materialistic temper of his successors, and with one or two experimental exceptions (as with Andrew Geddes), remained un-employed till the revival of etching in England under the auspices of Whistler and Seymour Haden.   Then it was once more well used, and it has continued ever since to be a part of the equipment of our fore-most etchers.

Dry-point is undoubtedly a noble medium for sketching.   Its lines have, individually, a richness and, when massed, a subtlety which no other materials so readily produce.   Yet the tone contrasts are so strong that care and experience are needed to prevent the effect becoming scattered or violent ; while the difficulty of rendering form precisely makes it (as we have already seen) unsuitable for some subjects, and for all who are not accomplished artists.   If used with genuine emotion, as was the case with Rembrandt, the most tremendous themes are not beyond its scope : if used without such emotion it may easily become theatrical or merely picturesque, as some clever modern French portraits indicate.   Its chief disad-vantage for serious work is the fact that only the first few proofs taken from the plate really show the full power of the medium.   Dry-point is thus an ex-travagant method to employ for an elaborate composi-tion, since the work will survive only in one or two dozen proofs, whereas, if executed in etching, it might be enjoyed by hundreds or thousands. The artist who makes the most generous use of his talent will therefore restrict his dry-point plates to subjects that appeal to the cultured few and the collectors of rare " states ": when working for a wider audience he will employ some form of engraving that, in the matter of reproduction, is less inexorably sterile.

MEZZOTINT

The majority of the processes of metal engraving involve working from light to dark, the untouched metal surface providing the lights, while the darks are produced by lines or spots cut into it. In mezzotint, as in wood engraving, the artist works from dark to light, the plate providing an uniform surface of shadow out of which the lights are cut. To produce the dark printing surface, the whole plate is mechanically roughened until it is covered with little evenly dis tributed teeth of metal which retain the ink. Where lights are required these teeth are cut away with a sharp steel scraper, or flattened out with a burnisher.

The rich luminous shadows obtained by the mezzotint process make it specially suitable for the reproduction of oil painting, and in that field mezzotint has achieved its chief triumphs. Almost at the moment of its invention, Prince Rupert produced his plate of *The*

Great Executioner after Spagnoletto which, in its way, has never been surpassed. The brilliant mezzotinters of the eighteenth century, who popularised the portraits of Reynolds, added new and subtle beauties to the craft, while, in the first half of the nineteenth century, it proved its fitness to deal with landscape in Turner's "Liber Studiorum," and in the delightful series of plates by David Lucas after Constable.

The tradition of the art is thus both splendid and varied. Yet in modern times it has attracted but few artists, except for reproductive purposes, and even by these has been but intermittently employed. Several reasons seem to have combined to produce this result. To begin with, the preparation of the toothed ground is somewhat costly: then the actual process of scraping is much slower and more laborious than it might seem at first sight, and it is apparently difficult to judge how far the work has progressed without taking frequent proofs from the plate. If the scraping is carried too far at any point, the engraver has to get a new ground laid and to work the passage again. Even the process of proving weakens the plate, since every proof that is taken wears away a little of the ground, and diminishes somewhat the richness of the effect. Mezzotint, too, produces the finest results when it renders deep shadows, and deep shadows are out of fashion. Possibly also original mezzotints do not appeal widely to collectors for the simple reason that there are no classical examples to serve as a standard, the few magnificent plates scraped by Turner being too rare to establish a precedent.

These extraordinary prints prove that mezzotint is as superb a medium for an original designer, as it was for the gifted men who reproduced the paintings of Reynolds or Constable, and that it possesses every important pictorial quality. The impossibility of rendering petty detail, and the possibility of veiling unessential portions of the design, are in themselves advantages which few other methods of painting or engraving can claim.

Its difficulties do not seem insuperable by practice and patience, and mezzotint would therefore appear to offer an almost virgin field to the first strenuous talent that has the courage to master it.

ETCHING

We may now come to the various methods in which the hollows in the metal plate, from which the printing ink is transferred to the paper, are produced by the corroding effect of an acid instead of being forcibly cut with a metal point. In the process of Etching, the metal plate is covered with a thin protective ground or varnish, upon which the design is drawn with a sharp needle. When acid is applied to the surface of the plate, it attacks the metal where it has been exposed by the passage of the point through the ground, and eats out U-shaped hollows, corresponding in size and depth to the breadth of the metal point, and to the time that the action of the acid is allowed to last. If the biting lasts but a short time the furrows will be shallow and the tint produced in printing will be faint ; if the acid is allowed to act for a long time the furrows will be deep, and the print from them will be strong. As it is easy to regulate the action of the acid on different parts of the same plate, varying degrees of depth corresponding to various degrees of tone can readily be produced.

These details are of slight importance compared with the advantage the medium possesses over other processes of engraving in the matter of facility. The metal point, if properly sharpened, meets with little or no resistance as it glides over the surface of the plate removing the varnish, and can thus be employed with a freedom analogous to that of a pen or pencil working on very smooth paper. The action of the acid, too, is slightly irregular, and gives the bitten line a ruggedness which is more picturesque than the severe precision of a line cut with the graver.

Etching thus combines the spirit and freedom of good pen work with a pleasant quality of substance which pen work lacks. It has also a great tradition beginning with Dürer and Rembrandt; indeed, the latter master carried the process so far, and developed it so nobly, that the achievement of the finest modern etchers is slight and limited in comparison. In one point, however, the great etchers agree, namely, that the power of the medium is shown most perfectly when reliance is placed upon the etched line, and upon that alone. The combination of a number of fine lines to form a tone has often been employed with consummate skill, both by Rembrandt, and by the clever moderns who used the process for engraving pictures, but the results are usually much inferior, both in force and vitality, to those obtained where the line is allowed to speak for itself, and tones are left out or but summarily suggested.

The pre-eminent virtue of an etched line, as of a pen line, is vitality. Hence the process is specially applicable to portraiture, to the sketching of figures in motion, to landscape, and to architecture. Moreover it is one of the few artistic processes commonly employed in Europe in which the omission of un-essential features is consistently illustrated and ap-proved by good tradition. It is thus a medium in which artistic emphasis can be readily attained, without demanding from the spectator a tithe of the under-standing or tolerance which he needs to possess when similar omissions and abstractions have not the comfortable assurance of tradition to back them.

No artist, perhaps, has explored the capacities of a medium so thoroughly as Rembrandt explored those of

L

etching, and in his mature plates deliberate omission is
carried further than in any other form of European
art previous to the nineteenth century.   In oil painting
he was unable to go so far, hence, magnificent as are
his paintings, many of the most masterly relics of
Rembrandt's genius are to be found in his etched
prints.   The conventions, nay, the very material of
his oil pictures, compelled the introduction of certain
unessentials, though he reduced them to a minimum.
In his etchings he was free to deal with essentials
alone.

Some ingenious moderns attempt to print etchings
in colour.   The result is, at best, a sorry substitute for
painting, while the colouring deprives the medium of
the abstract quality to which its greatest manifestations owe their excellence.   It is just because the
etched line does not imitate nature that its lively
suggestiveness is so infinite in scope.

Yet the quality of infinity is not easily or often
obtained in etching.   The character of the etched line,
with all its picturesqueness, is clear and precise, and
the character of an etched print is apt to be clear and
precise also.   Hence in these days we have perhaps
three hundred clever etchers, and perhaps thirty who
might be termed powerful or brilliant, but hardly three
who can be said to extend their expression beyond the
range of positive facts.   Yet for all great work this
extension is indispensable.   In the case of etching

extreme subtlety of drawing will do much, especially in the case of portraiture, as the example of Van Dyck proves. Subtlety of chiaroscuro is, however, the more obvious way of escape from prosiness, and here the varied resources of biting, the mixture of delicate lines with strong ones may come to the etcher's aid.

Rembrandt himself came more and more to depend upon dry-point as an accessory to, or even as a substitute for the bitten line; Goya reinforced line with aquatint; Whistler and other moderns have refined their effects by skilful wiping of the plate before printing. Other devices will be found in the hand-books on the subject. Unless an etching is very large or very unevenly bitten, it can hardly lack unity, or sin very grievously from lack of repose, while the process of steel-facing permits hundreds of proofs to be taken from a single plate without any very serious loss of quality. Altogether no artistic medium at present in use deserves its popularity better.

AQUATINT

In etching proper the metal plate is covered with an uniform coat of resinous varnish. In aquatint the resin is applied in the form of small separate particles. When the prepared surface is exposed to the action of acid, the acid eats away the copper which is left bare in the interstices between the grains of resin. The reticulation thus produced on the copper, prints as a tint corresponding in darkness to the period of exposure to the acid, and in evenness to the minuteness of the grains of resin. A similar grain of a coarser kind may be obtained by pressing sand- or emery-paper into an ordinary etching ground, and then biting the broken surface. Work in aquatint is conducted by stopping the action of the acid where lights are required by covering these portions with varnish ; for darker passages this stopping out is delayed, while the deepest darks of all are produced by a long exposure.

The flat tints thus obtained are naturally quiet and harmonious, but it is difficult to get forcible effects without coarseness, and almost impossible, apparently, to get subtlety, detail, or fine contours. Possibly these deficiencies account for the fact that aquatint pure and simple has not, I think, been used by any great artist. Goya has employed it with magnificent effect in combination with etching, the bitten line supplying the accent, the detail, and the precise contours which aquatint lacks. A few modern etchers, too, have produced good results on similar lines. Some French engravers of the eighteenth century, such as Grateloup, seem to have possessed a mastery of a process, of which the result is indistinguishable from incredibly fine aquatint. It is possible that a patient student might rediscover their secret and extend indefinitely its employment for artistic purposes. Yet since the use of aquatint in connection with etching is still but half explored, this would seem a more promising line of research. Many English landscape aquatints of the eighteenth century are not without a certain grandeur, heavy, clumsy, or empty though they are commonly apt to be. Could something of their breadth and spaciousness be allied to the spirit and precision of the etched line, aquatint would deserve a new lease of life.

CHAPTER XIII

WATER-COLOUR AND TEMPERA PAINTING

THE processes of applying pigment to any surface for the purpose of making a picture may be classified according to the mediums with which the pigments are mixed; and the process of painting with the simplest of all mediums, pure water, may well take precedence of more complicated methods. For practical purposes the forms of water-colour painting may be classified under three heads:

1. Transparent water colour, in which the colours are simply mixed with water, and depend for their luminosity upon a white ground which shows through the thin washes of pigment.

2. Body colour, in which the colours are mixed with a solid opaque white, usually zinc white.

3. A mixed method in which both transparent colour and opaque colour are used side by side.

The effects produced by these three methods of work are radically different so that it is impossible to deal with them together.

TRANSPARENT WATER COLOUR

Though the tradition of transparent water colour in its more complicated forms is largely an English tradition, the method was in general use long before English artists had attained to definite rank. The most precious relics of this early use of the medium are the drawings of Claude and Rembrandt. In these the water-colour work is almost always in monochrome, and is generally employed to soften and complete a drawing made with the pen. The method is one of singular power and beauty. The pen lines give structure, backbone and natural lively emphasis to the design. The wash of bistre or Indian ink softens the asperity of the pen strokes, and supplements their force by suggesting texture and tone.

Of the two artists Rembrandt is the more direct, and his superb sketches seem for the most part to have been invented and finished in a single brief sitting. The methods of Claude are more elaborate, the strength of his pen lines being often modified by washing with water, and the atmospheric effect of the distances being sometimes enhanced by a direct use of opaque white, the contrast of this clouded pigment with the transparent portions of the drawing at times giving a delightful suggestion of actual colour, analogous to that found in the sketches of Gainsborough. This combination of pen and wash was commonly employed by the later

Italians for studies of figure compositions, and very cleverly; but with the decay of their fame the method fell into disuse and has never been seriously revived till our own time—possibly because the practice of water-colour painting with a full palette came into notice at the beginning of the nineteenth century, and has held men's attention ever since.

Yet the method of pen and wash drawing deserves to be remembered. Its record from the days of Rembrandt and Claude to those of Turner's studies for the "Liber Studiorum" is one of singular excellence. If it cannot pretend to imitate the colouring of nature, it has at any rate proved itself well fitted to suggest many of her most enchanting effects. It is not perhaps so perfectly adapted for the study of the human figure as hard chalk, since it cannot be gradated with quite the same certainty, and therefore the skill of a Rembrandt is needed to use it with success in drawing from the nude. Its value however for rapid notation of effects of light and shade is unequalled, and thus it should be specially useful to the landscape painter. For landscape too it has a fitness which is shared by all other monochrome processes.

The colour of landscape is often unpictorial, if not actually unpleasing, at the very moment when the forms and the light and shade are most effectively disposed. We may see, for instance, a building of raw brick set upon fresh green grass with a glaring blue sky behind, which has nevertheless a certain dignity either momentary or intrinsic. To sit down and paint the scene as we see it would clearly result in a disagreeable picture ; yet to wait till twilight, when the tones of earth and architecture and sky blend more happily, may be impossible, or may involve the loss of the very effect of lighting upon which the interest of the subject hangs. By making a sketch in pen and wash, we are able to get from the subject just the elements of form and shadow that constitute its pictorial beauty, and dispense with the colour which introduces the jarring note. As previously mentioned the omission of local colour has the additional advantage of increasing the luminosity of the lighter portions of the drawing, so that the monochrome sketch will not only be more harmonious than a coloured one, but more brilliant and effective as well.

A full palette of water-colour has been also used in combination with pen work, but much less frequently than Indian ink or bistre. For landscape it was employed by Philips de Koninck, who thus got effects rather more like nature, from a chromatic point of view, than those of his master Rembrandt, but far less luminous and majestic. Other Dutch masters, of whom Van Ostade is the most notable, made pen drawings of figure subjects which they tinted with washes of colour, producing results that were often lively and pleasant. Their example was freely followed both on the Continent and in England, where the genius of Rowlandson extracted from the process the most artistic results which have been attained with it hitherto.

Rowlandson wisely confined himself to a few simple tints which he used with great judgment as accessories to his masterly pen work, usually more with the view of adding an element of charm to drawings already overflowing with force and spirit, than of increasing their emphasis. On occasion, of course, Rowlandson could make his colour as significant as his drawing, but his customary practice has been that adopted by the clever illustrators of the latter half of the nineteenth century, and only one or two artists in our own day have attempted to put the method to more serious use. The foundation of pen lines can give both unity and vitality to all work thus executed, and reasonable taste in the colouring will secure repose. If the quality of infinity is to be obtained at all it also must be obtained chiefly from the colour, for it is there that the method seems most elastic. Some help too may be derived from the planning and spacing which, since the work will usually be upon a small scale, can with safety be made much bolder and more capricious than is pleasing in the case of a large picture.

In water colour proper the washes of colour are laid directly on the paper, usually over a faint pencil outline. A considerable number of water-colour studies of this type have been left by the Dutch and Flemish masters, sometimes, as with Cuyp, verging upon monochrome, at others, as with Dürer, Van Dyck, and Jordaens, admitting the occasional use of body colour, and approaching our modern methods of sketching both in vividness and in treatment.

These masters, however, were the forerunners of our modern tradition rather than its founders, and the true origin of the water-colour drawing of to-day, must be referred to the stained drawing of the eighteenth century. In these drawings, originally intended for engravers, a pencil outline was first reinforced by washes of Indian ink: then, on the top of this monochrome drawing, a limited number of pale tints were laid, so that the result was at least suggestive of nature's colouring. The finest and most typical specimens of this method of work are to be found in such drawings as those of John Robert Cozens. The method was admirably adapted for the expression of space, atmosphere and tranquillity, but forcible effects, either of colour or of light and shade, were beyond its scope. Thus, while equipped with the other qualities of good pictorial art, the stained drawing is apt to be deficient in vitality, and though a great artist might overcome this weakness it none the less limits the employment of the method to a somewhat narrow range of subjects.

Girtin is said (on no very conclusive evidence)

to have been the first to emancipate draughtsmen from this thraldom, by working in pure colour without a monochrome foundation, and upon his death the change was completed by Turner, Constable, Cox, De Wint, and Cotman. Turner, after inventing or perfecting most of the technical devices on which the water-colour artist of to-day depends for getting variety of texture, gradually gave up the study of chiaroscuro for that of colour, of which he became a remarkable exponent. No other water-colour artist has equalled him in the boldness with which he combined the most brilliant tints, or has employed them with so small a sacrifice of luminosity. He had learned early in life that water colour was preeminently the medium of tricks and dodges, by which effects could be produced that were quite beyond the reach of straightforward manipulation, and his unremitting activity soon gave him a varied facility in their employment which it is improbable that any artist in the future will quite attain.

Constable and Cox also began work upon the lines of Girtin, but their natural instinct was for sunlight, fresh air, and movement. To suggest them they invented formulæ of their own, symbolising the vibration of light and the movement of clouds, grass, and trees, by broken touches, in place of the broad level washes beloved of their predecessors. De Wint's talent was devoted to effects of deep rich colour, and though too frequently wasted on the production of pretty finished drawings, achieved enough broad and masterly sketches to entitle him to a high place among our leading water-colourists. Cotman's great natural gifts were warped by the necessity of teaching, and the touch of the drawing master is too often apparent in his work. Yet both in design and colour he was an innovator, whose drawings, even when they are least successful, aim at an ideal of style which our realistic age is not constituted to appreciate at its full value. The coming of the Pre-raphaelites introduced a desire for more minute detail, and more literal resemblance to the tones and colours of nature, a desire which our prominent water-colourists attempted to satisfy up to our own time. Recently the Impressionist painters have led artists to think more about sunlight and less about finish.

Each of these demands has in turn been met by the water-colour medium, but when we look back at the total result, it proves just a little disappointing. We have many clever and brilliant sketches, but comparatively few notable works of art. For sketching indeed, no process has perhaps so many obvious merits as water-colour drawing. It is simple and rapid in manipulation, it renders delicate tones with ease, and it is not devoid of force in rendering full ones ; no other process is so rich in felicitous accident, so crisp and fresh in character, or better fitted if the need arises for rendering minute detail. It is hardly wonderful that so useful a medium should be popular both with painters and the public: yet it has not satisfied exacting critics.

It is easy to attribute this dissatisfaction to prejudice contracted from long acquaintance with oil and tempera painting, but such prejudice, even if it existed, would not be a complete explanation. We all recognise that water colours cannot, as a rule, be seen to advantage among oil or tempera paintings. That recognition in itself may not prove that water colour is inferior to oil painting in every respect, or under all circumstances. Some water colours indeed stand the ordeal well; but the great majority undoubtedly look weak in tone and poor in quality under such conditions, and the inferiority is seen so often that we are compelled to inquire whether some inherent weakness in the medium may not be responsible for it.

The truth seems to be that the ordinary transparent water-colour drawing, while it may suggest beautiful things, is not itself beautiful in substance, and this lack of beauty of substance is accentuated by the fact that it is executed in colour. An etching or a drawing in black chalk may not possess actual beauty of material, but since it is mere black and white, the absence of beauty does not force itself upon us. The introduction of colour makes all the difference. Colour cannot be a neutral quantity. When it is not positively good it is bad, and in water-colour drawing it is often difficult to get really good colour. Compared with the effects produced by other mediums its tones seem to be either feeble or thin, or hard or dull. When they aim at the exquisite cool-ness of fresco and tempera they commonly succeed in being no more than poor and cold; when they aim at the richness of oil paint they become garish and heavy.

The primary cause of this poorness of quality seems to reside in the transparency of the thin wash of pigment, and in the uniform luminosity of the paper beneath to which the colour owes its brightness. Its failings in fact are similar to those of the modern stained glass windows which are made of glass that is too evenly transparent. The old glass was far more uneven in quality; it was trans-parent in some places, nearly opaque elsewhere, and to the varied vibrancy caused by these inequalities it owes its peculiar richness of effect. The water-colourist is confronted by a similar problem, which the great artists who have used the medium have solved, either by modifying the transparency of their washes through the introduction of semi-opaque pig-ment, or, while retaining transparency, have prevented it from becoming monotonous by manipulating the surface beneath. For the moment we are concerned only with the second of these processes.

Occasionally the paper itself supplies the needful variety. That, for example, which Girtin preferred appears to have been semi-absorbent, and the washes of colour instead of merely resting on the surface of the sheet became actually incorporated with it. The drawings executed under these conditions have a pleasant "matt" quality which is not found in subsequent work, although in our own time a not unsuccessful effort has been made to revive the manufacture of a slightly absorbent paper, like that used at the close of the eighteenth century. The artists of China and Japan escaped this difficulty by working upon silk, a ground which in Europe has so far been used only by fan-painters.

Another method of getting variety of surface was the employment of papers which were not pure white, but were granulated or tinted with some neutral colour. Granulated papers often gave good results, but were rarely of good quality. They might serve well for rapid sketches, but were often unsuitable for prolonged or delicate working. Besides, being usually made of poor materials, they were open to suspicion in the matter of permanence. Tinted papers could be made of good materials, and equal in other respects to the best white paper, and so were largely employed during the middle of the nineteenth century; but the mechanical tinting was too regular and, though it tended to deaden tones which might otherwise have been too violent, it did not sensibly improve the quality of the water-colour washes.

The employment of a very rough paper was perhaps more successful. It served at least to give variety of surface, and, where it was employed for rapid sketching (its proper field, since the roughness precludes minute drawing of detail), there was a tendency for the brush to leave little spots and dots of white paper uncovered. These introduced a certain freshness and sparkle to the work which is not inappropriate to breezy landscape subjects of the type first developed by David Cox.

The rawness of white paper was also decreased by a preliminary wash of faint colour, usually of a warm yellow tone, though in some cases Indian ink appears to have been used with very good effect. Such a wash indeed, would seem to be much preferable to the use of a tinted paper. If properly applied it would have just those slight variations of tone and quality which mechanical tinting lacks, and would therefore be a better foundation for subsequent washes of colour.

We may now turn to the devices employed for improving the effect of water-colour drawing by treatment after the washes of colour have been applied. The most important of these is the device of wiping out lights, by first damping the surface and then rubbing it with a rag, bread-crumbs or india-rubber. This practice, if not invented by Turner, was first

M

employed systematically by him. The rubbing not only produces a variety of surface texture but, if it be not too roughly treated, the rubbed portion retains a faint suggestion of its original hue. The device thus makes for variety both of texture and quality, and so becomes a valuable addition to the resources of the medium.

Large surfaces are often treated by sponging or prolonged washing. Turner is said to have left his drawings in water for hours together when he desired exceptional delicacy. Great evenness of tone may be produced by such means, but the freshness and strength of the colour is usually sacrificed, so that the result is apt to be dull or feeble in effect, as we see in the case of Copley Fielding, who seems to have relied very frequently upon sponging and washing.

A method used by Cotman gives better results. He often seems to have worked in flat tones upon moderately rough paper. Then when the washes were dry, a damp cloth was passed over the surface once or twice. This removed particles of colour from the projecting portions of the paper, but left the colour in the hollows untouched, and the work acquired thereby a not unpleasant texture. Tradition also states that the forcible effects Cotman produced were sometimes due to the use of sour paste to strengthen the body of his colours, and to allow of a manipulation .resembling in some degree that of painting in oil.

Scraping with a sharp knife was also employed, both to modify texture, and to get sharp glittering lights. The later water-colours of Constable afford many instances of the practice, but it demands considerable skill on the part of the draughtsman, and it is not so generally applicable as "wiping out" or rubbing with a damp cloth.

One device now rarely employed may also be mentioned, namely, that of stopping out. The lights of a drawing were painted in spirit varnish. The drawing was then made, the tints where necessary being carried boldly over the varnish. The varnish was next dissolved, and the white uncoloured spaces came into view, to be re-worked or left as circumstances demanded. The effect was somewhat similar to that obtained by body colour, but the complexity of the process was doubtless the cause of its failure to find more general favour.

The method of stippling, by which the washes are reinforced with small touches of pure colour placed side by side, was used with great frequency and subtlety by Turner. He produced remarkably brilliant effects of colour with it, especially when the stippling was confined to the focus of interest, and when it was contrasted with the more even tones produced by washing. The moment stipple is used all over the surface of a drawing it loses its usefulness and becomes a fault: a petty touch is substituted for broad handling, and little strokes, which would have given variety of texture and surface had they been used with moderation, become more monotonous than the simple washes which they cover. Stippling is thus a method only for powerful and practised artists. In feeble hands it is an incitement to additional feebleness.

MIXED METHODS OF WATER COLOUR

Though the beauty of an unsullied wash of water colour upon certain kinds of paper is great, that beauty is not always at the artist's command, if only for the reason that a perfect paper of the kind required is rarely to be found, nor does the beauty obtained in this way fit every subject or every kind of decorative need. It is an austere and simple beauty which cannot be allied either with opulent effects of colour, with extreme subtlety of modelling, or with intricate design. If such things are needed, transparent water colour can only render them, where it can render them at all, with the assistance of devices such as wiping out and stippling.

The possibility of strengthening the painter's resources by the use of opaque pigment, in addition to the transparent washes, was recognised at an early date, and the combination of the two methods (as we have seen) is illustrated to advantage in many of the drawings of Claude, where the use of opaque white.

in the background of drawings executed chiefly in pen and bistre wash, gives the distance a quality of opalescent colour and a suggestion of atmosphere which could not have been attained so readily by any other means.

The same device was taken up by Gainsborough and used with even more conspicuous succcess. His landscape and figure drawings are infinitely various in their technical resource, but the best of them depend for their aerial beauty upon a combination of processes, in which black chalk, used directly or with the stump, upon a toned paper, is united with touches of other chalk, and of colours both transparent and opaque. Sometimes after the design has been laid in lightly with chalk, the whole is united with a wash of wet transparent colour, and the result is reinforced when dry by further work with chalk or opaque colour. At other times the design seems to have been worked with chalk or brush into a preparation of wet opaque colour. The methods employed produce such a variety of delightful results, that Gainsborough's drawings might well be as much studied by artists as they are now sought for by collectors.

In the hands of his less sensitive successors at the beginning of the nineteenth century the obvious features of Gainsborough's method were reduced to a system, and the practice of drawing on a toned paper in pencil or black chalk, and then adding high lights

with body colour or white chalk, became the stereo-
typed formula of teaching art to amateurs. The
method was too fine to deserve such degradation. The
tone of the ground gave unity and repose, the chalk
drawing gave vitality, while the mixture of transparent and opaque colour gave subtlety. Even when
black chalk is used as a foundation for transparent
water colour on white paper, the process of washing
incorporates small portions of the chalk with the
colour, and mitigates any tendency to harshness.

Both for the realistic Orientalism of J. F. Lewis and
for the glowing romanticism of Rossetti, brilliant colour
was essential. Lewis, the less influential and important of the two, mingled body colour and transparent colour with singular felicity, and seems to have
got every effect he wanted with no more help than that
of miraculous precision of touch and keenness of eyesight. The masterly water colours of Rossetti display
a still wider range of technical resource, every device
known to the water-colourist being pressed into
service, and used with the utmost possible freedom.
To obtain variety of hue and texture, Rossetti, without
the least hesitation, mixed opaque colour with transparent (though he did not use opaque colour to the
same extent as Lewis), washed, scraped, or cut away
the surface of his paper, and then stippled over the
irregularities so produced, at times almost seeming to
carve his work rather than to paint it.

The result, in Rossetti's best period, is a series of small drawings which are no less rich in quality and forcible in hue than they are profound in feeling and superb in concentrated design. In them and in a few drawings by other men, such as Burne-Jones working under Rossetti's immediate influence, water colour attains a perfection similar to that which, in a different field, was attained by Turner. The method of Turner, however, with all its variety, relies largely upon broad washes of colour, and is thus best suited to the wide expanse of earth and sky for which he employed it The method of Rossetti is pre-eminently that of a colourist in the full and fervent key of a Titian, and so is the more suitable for subjects in which figures play a predominant part. Figure pieces executed in transparent colour may be pretty but, with very few exceptions, they are feeble and anæmic products when carried beyond the stage of a rapid sketch. Even though our annual exhibitions continue to be crowded with examples of this kind of figure-work, and the exhibitors are sometimes wonderfully skilful, no technical accomplishment can quite prevail over the inherent weakness of the transparent method for treating such subjects, and the student will be wise to carry out his figure drawings on the lines of Rossetti and the Pre-raphaelites, or take frankly to body colour.

OPAQUE METHODS OF WATER COLOUR

The art of painting in opaque colour has been practised both in Europe and the East for many centuries.
In China and Japan it has been consistently used for
important pictures ; in India and Persia, as well as in
Europe, it was chiefly employed for miniatures and for
illuminated books.   The earlier Persian illuminated
manuscripts rival our most famous European volumes:
their portraits are of equal beauty, though the miniatures of Holbein and Nicholas Hilliard remain, in their
particular field, unsurpassed.   The finest examples of
Samuel Cooper alone can stand any comparison with
them, and the comparison only serves to show the
advantage of opaque over transparent colour for miniature work.   It has the property of remaining cool and
blonde in quality even when rendering the most vivid
hues, and thus keeps a pleasant texture and surface ·
where transparent colour of the same brightness would
inevitably be garish.   Drawings like those of Mr. Sargent suffer from this defect.   It cannot render depth of
shadow well, but as Hilliard himself has pointed out in
his " Treatise on the Art of Limning," depth of shadow
is unessential in miniatures.   The point may well be
worth attention in these days, when the tradition of
miniature oscillates between faint memories of the
prettiness of Cosway and baleful competition with
tinted photographs.   The revival of the art of illumina_

tion, due to the influence of William Morris, suggests that a similar revival of miniature on the lines of Holbein and Hilliard would not be impossible. The comparative inaccessibility of the finest originals is the chief drawback the student has to face, for nothing short of the originals will convey any just idea of their beauty.

Body colour was occasionally employed by the later artists of the Renaissance, and in eighteenth-century England the name of Paul Sandby is conspicuous among its patrons, but few of the drawings executed before the time of Turner have any serious claims to notice. Turner revolutionised the opaque method, as he did those of transparent water colour and of oil painting, and his sketches for the Rivers of France series rank among the most uniformly successful of his many achievements.

His usual practice was to work on a grayish blue paper, over which he spread a thin wash of opaque colour into which the stronger tints were worked. Sometimes this foundation tint plays a large part in the general scheme; at others it is veiled by subsequent painting. The colouring of the sketches executed in this manner is uniformly rich, forcible and luminous, and in point of surface texture and general pictorial quality they leave nothing to be desired. The underlying tone of gray knits together any parts of the composition that might tend to separate from the rest,

and harmonises the most daring contrasts of colour.
One who has made copies of many of these Turner
drawings for Ruskin informs me that the washes and
touches of body colour throughout are very much
thinner than their appearance suggests. To this the
tints doubtless owe their vibrancy and lightness.

Of recent years body colour has been employed
with success for landscape work by some of our most
gifted artists, while in France it is among the methods
employed by Degas and other famous masters. In
the hands of Mr. Conder silk instead of paper is used
as a ground, and the colour effects produced in his
fans and panels are among the most notable achievements of our time. Linen also is sometimes used with
success.

Body colour, indeed, is a colourist's medium, and
though the example of Holbein and the great illumi-
nators has proved that superb colour is not incompatible with minute finish, the best results produced
by the method in modern times are invariably loose
and broad in handling. On any scale but that of a
miniature, high finish seems to result in heaviness. By
adopting a loose treatment in body-colour work, the
artist is able to avail himself of another advantage, and
that no small one, which the method possesses. In
few other processes is the omission of unnecessary
detail so easy. When once the essential features of
the design are stated, the brown or gray ground,

whether it be left untouched or be covered with a preliminary wash of colour, makes a perfect support for
them, without suggesting to the spectator the feeling
of emptiness which is conveyed by white paper or
untouched canvas. The slightest sketch in body
colour has, in fact, a sort of decorative completeness
which in other mediums can be obtained, if at all, only
with labour and experience.

This advantage is doubtless accountable for the
popularity of body colour with the artists of China
and Japan, who have realised for centuries that the
artist is recognised as much by what he leaves out of
his pictures as by what he puts into them. Their art
is far more symbolical than our own and its symbolism
is of a kind which few Occidentals can hope to understand; but it is always pre-eminently artistic in its
disdain of unessential things, a disdain which such
mediums as body colour and lacquer enable it to gratify.

TEMPERA PAINTING

For details of the process of painting in tempera by
which were produced the easel pictures of the early
Italian masters, and therefore some of the most exquisite
works of art in the world, the student must refer to the
various treatises on the subject, among which Mrs. Her-
ringham's translation of Cennino Cennini's " Trattato "
is the most complete and accessible. The essence of

the process is the use of yolk of egg diluted with water, as a painting vehicle. This vehicle is ground up with the dry powdered colours, and they are thinned with it to the degree necessary for convenient manipulation. The ground is usually one of fine white gesso applied either to panel or to canvas.

The technique of tempera is rendered entirely different from that of other forms of painting by the fact that the colours dry almost immediately. It is thus impossible to obtain fusion and modelling by blending one touch with its predecessor; the touches can only be laid side by side or superposed. It follows that a tempera painting has to be built up by a number of successive strokes and hatchings, which may indeed be slightly modified by a rapid wash of thin colour, but the style will always remain to some extent linear. Alterations, too, are almost impossible, and a design cannot be amended after the work has once been well started.

The peculiar qualities of tempera are the pearly translucency of its tints, and the general luminosity of its tone. It is therefore able to render pale shades of blue and gray and lilac, which in oil paintings would become chalky; a faculty to which the skies and distances of the early masters owe their tranquil charm. Tempera would thus seem specially adapted to many of those cool, open-air effects which modern landscape artists find peculiarly difficult.

That it is not more frequently employed for such subjects must be attributed to two reasons. In the first place the rapid drying makes the touch precise, so that the artist is debarred from the freedom of handling which working in wet colour permits. This is particularly needed in landscape both to express rapid movement, and to suggest what may be termed the accidental element in nature.

Tempera too is not intrinsically a forcible method of work for deep tones and strong shadows have to be built up by repeated washings or hatchings. On this ground it was ultimately superseded in Italy by oil painting. At first pigments ground in oil were used as a kind of varnish to enrich tempera. Gradually this finishing process became more important than the tempera work, underneath; so that, in the pictures of the youthful Titian and his earlier Venetian contemporaries, we find the tempera painting is a mere foundation or ground for the elaborate work in oil which is executed over it. Probably a large part of the so-called " Venetian secret " of painting consisted merely in the use of a luminous tempera ground under the rich oil pigment with which the main portion of the work was carried out.

It is unlikely that tempera will again come into general use until some and ready means has been found for retarding the rapid drying of the colours, so that a fusion of tones may be obtained more readily than by the laborious process of cross-hatching. Were this disadvantage once removed, its advantages for many kinds of work would be considerable, since the preparation of the gesso ground offers no great difficulty, and the peculiar qualities obtained by tempera are admirably suited to more than one class of painting.

The method which was employed for such a masterpiece as Michelangelo's unfinished *Entombment*, in the National Gallery, is evidently not unfitted for the greatest and gravest subjects. Absolute certainty of design may still be a necessity, effects of swift motion may still be difficult to suggest, and forcible chiaroscuro may still be beyond its scope, but for serious figure composition, where the mood is restful and the purpose decorative, tempera in the future may prove the best of all mediums. For certain phases of Alpine landscape, where clear definition, brilliant light and brilliant colour are essential, it has already proved its usefulness, and its scope for landscape work might be vastly extended if the drying of the pigment could be delayed.

Of the four pictorial conditions, unity and repose are the two which tempera most readily fulfils, from the fact that strong contrasts of tone are not easily produced. Reasonable coherence of plan, and reasonable agreement between the chief colours employed, are all that the artist need secure for his work to look both compact and restful. Infinity must be sought for in delicate gradation of hue, tone and contour; for a rough workman, the suggestive and accidental processes of oil or water colour will prove more suitable. Vitality, however, is the quality for which the tempera painter will have the hardest struggle, since the natural tendency of the medium is to be calm, cool and static. Movement cannot be suggested in tempera as it is suggested by a rapid blot in water colour, or by a rapid scribble with a pen. Tempera is precise and deliberate, so the impression of life and vigour has to be conveyed by forcible planning, or by vivid modelling of the human figure,* helped out by stimulating contrasts in the colour which, in the absence of strong tones, becomes the most effective means of getting emphasis. So much is this the case, that the painter who is not sure of his power as a colourist would be wise to leave tempera alone.

* Mr. Berenson's well-known hand-book, "The Florentine Painters of the Renaissance," contains a brilliant and interesting analysis of the Florentine sense of the "tactile values" of the human figure, which renders unnecessary any further discussion of the subject in this place.

CHAPTER XIV

OIL PAINTING: THE TRANSPARENT METHOD

By mixing powder colours with a siccative oil or varnish, a pigment is produced which may be practically permanent when applied to a variety of surfaces, which lends itself readily to manipulation with the brush, and which is capable of much solidity, force and richness of effect. The process of oil painting has thus become the method by which pictures of any size and importance are most commonly produced in Europe. So many, however, are the forms which oil painting may assume, and so different are the results obtained in each case, that it is impossible to deal with all these variations as if they were one and the same process. Every great artist has developed some portion or portions of these numerous qualities till his method has become a thing distinct in itself, and a complete study of the tradition of oil painting could only be carried out by making a series of detailed tudies of the various great paintings produced by it. For practical purposes, however, it will be sufficient to classify the innumerable ways of using oil paint under three general headings.

1. The transparent method, in which the pigments are used thinly, and depend chiefly or entirely for their effect upon light reflected from a luminous ground ; as in the work of the early Flemish masters in the past, and of the Pre-raphaelites and Mr. Orchardson in our own day.

2. The mixed method, which depends partly upon light reflected from the ground, and partly upon light reflected from a solid body of pigment. This has been in general use with mature schools of art from the early part of the sixteenth century till the latter part of the nineteenth.

3. The opaque method, which depends entirely upon light reflected from a solid body of pigment: an entirely modern invention introduced to public notice by the so-called Impressionists.

Painting with oil or varnish upon a gesso ground had been practised long before the days of the brothers Van Eyck, more especially in Northern Europe, where the dampness of the climate necessitated a stronger vehicle to preserve the colours than was required in Italy. The ground was usually of gesso, similar to that prepared for tempera painting, but the oleo-resinous vehicles employed were neither colourless nor, it would seem, easy to manipulate. The " inven

N

tion " of Hubert and John Van Eyck was the discovery
of a medium that was at once permanent, colourless,
and capable of rendering accurately the most minute
detail.

Their painting was in principle similar to glass
painting, in that the transparent tints were illuminated
by light shining through them. To attain the most
brilliant results, every care was taken to ensure first
of all that the ground was a brilliant white, which would
reflect every possible atom of light which fell upon it
through the thin pigment. Well-prepared gesso, rendered unabsorbent to avoid the risk of staining, gave
this brightness, and was laid on panels much more
frequently than on canvas.

No less care was given to the pigments, and the
vehicle used to apply and preserve them, perfect
clearness and transparency being the ideals, so that
the colours when spread over the white ground might
have the luminous and gem-like quality of fine stained
glass. The unfinished picture of *St. Barbara* by John
Van Eyck in the Antwerp Gallery shows clearly how the
Flemish masters worked. The design was first carefully drawn on the gesso ground, perfect in all its
details, and the painting was then executed piece by
piece, each part being finished before the next was
started. The panel was sometimes toned with a wash
of pale colour, often a flesh tint, before the actual
painting w as started. This tone served to fix the

lines of the drawing, and to modify the extreme white-
ness of the gesso. When finished the painting was
exposed to the sun, not so much to dry the pigment,
as to extract the excess of oil, which otherwise would
have accumulated near the surface in course of time,
and would have given the work a yellowish tone.

The bleaching action of sunlight upon the oils used
in painting is not always remembered. Yet the letters
of Rubens, were other evidence wanting, make it
plain that this bleaching was an essential part of
Northern technique. The oils used in painting, however carefully they may be clarified and refined, tend
with the lapse of years to rise to the surface of a
painting and form a semi-resinous coating of brown
or yellow, which may preserve the pigments underneath, but certainly darkens their tone and destroys
their freshness. The painter is thus compelled to get
rid of every superfluous atom of oil in his picture, if
he wishes it to retain its pristine brightness.

The transparent method of oil painting practically
implied the use of colour in a liquid state, so that the
amount of oil would have been a serious danger if no
steps had been taken to remove it. The practice of
exposing pictures to sunshine was a perfect remedy
for the disease; indeed, if the sunning be continued
long enough it is said to remove the oil so completely
that the work assumes the dry matt surface and
quality of tempera. If continued only for a reasonable

time it not only removes the superfluous oil, but under favourable conditions leaves the picture with a smooth enamelled surface, which makes varnishing unnecessary. So brilliant, indeed, does the effect sometimes become that one is tempted to wonder whether the medium of the Van Eycks contained any varnish at all, and whether their results were not produced simply with linseed oil and sunshine. An absorbent ground was occasionally tried in later times, so that the oil might sink down into the gesso instead of rising to the surface, but with no good result. The oil stained the gesso and destroyed its brightness, while, owing to the absorption from below, it had to be used in much greater quantities, so that the remedy in the end proved worse than the disease.

In Italy the process of painting was much simplified by natural causes. In the first place the general dryness of the climate made it unnecessary to preserve pigments from damp by locking them up with a quantity of oil and varnish. A thinner and more volatile medium (such as Venice turpentine dissolved in an essential oil) was commonly used. This dried "matt", and the picture was completed with a coat of amber or other varnish. Even when linseed oil was used, the warmth of the Italian climate rendered the process of sunning very short, so that the Italians had not to take the same precautions against yellowing that were required north of the Alps. The works of our

own painter, Richard Wilson, are an excellent illustra·
tion of the difference. His early landscapes painted
in the warm dry Italian air are fresh and bright; his
later pictures painted in the dark and foggy atmo
sphere of London are always yellowish, because the
linseed oil which he used has never been dried out of
them.

In Northern Europe the method of the Van Eycks
was applied to a much wider range of subjects than
they had attempted, by masters like the elder Bruegel
and Dürer; the former, indeed, using it with a raci-
ness and vigour which prepared the way for Rubens.
The practice of Rubens differed from that of his forerunners in more than one respect. On the white
ground he laid in a complete chiaroscuro study in transparent brown, so strong in tone that its shadows
would serve for the shadows of the subsequent painting.
Over this the colours were laid thinly, except in the
lights and the half-lights, where opaque pigment was
used in considerable body. His method in this respect was just the contrary of that of the early masters.
Their lights, being obtained by a slight tinting of the
luminous ground, were the thinnest part of their
pictures, while their shadows were often the thickest.

Among the Dutch painters Teniers may be mentioned as a consistent worker on the principle of
Rubens, but Rembrandt and most of the other masters,
although they use transparent colour freely, use opaque

colours with equal freedom, and what I have termed the mixed method became the established way of painting in oil. Not until we come to the landscapes of Gainsborough do we see a notable revival of transparent work.

The change that was effected slowly in Northern Europe came about much more rapidly in the South. In spite of the interest created by the Flemish method of oil painting when it was first popularised in Italy by Antonello da Messina, it seems to have been rarely or never employed by other Italian artists, except as a means of enriching a design already begun in tempera. With the artists of the ripe Renaissance the tempera foundation was dispensed with ; but at the same time the use of opaque and semi-opaque pigments became general.

Thus in the Venetian School we find the exquisite transparent oil painting of the time of John Bellini and the young Giorgione, executed upon a tempera ground. The tempera ground survives in the later work of Giorgione, and in the early work of Titian, but there, already, we see the use of opaque and semi-opaque colours creeping in ; till, in the mature work of Titian, the painting becomes so solid that the luminous ground plays quite a subordinate part, or is entirely hidden.

When we ask ourselves how this delightful mode of painting, with its unique charm of gem-like colour, and those qualities of limpidity and precision which make the works of its earlier practitioners among the most delightful of the world's art products, came to be super-seded all over Europe, the answer is not far to seek.

The beauties of the Flemish method were accom-panied with certain limitations which made it unsuit-able to the taste of the full Renaissance. It was essentially a method for small panels: the sixteenth century required large decorative canvases. It made alterations in design unsatisfactory if not impossible: the sixteenth century demanded a less inelastic method, affording facilities for free improvisation. Its capacity, too, for delicate detail was unaccompanied by a capacity for suggesting varieties of texture equal to that of solid pigment: while its exquisite rendering of transparent air left it still unable to represent the mysterious vaporous effects of atmosphere which an age bent on realism had discovered.

Realism, in fact, was responsible for the discarding of the Flemish method. It could delineate facts, but for interpreting the broad effects of nature's air and sunshine, and for suggesting the solidity and texture of natural substances, translucent or opaque colours were convenient, quite apart from the increased breadth of handling that their employment seemed to place within the painter's reach. As frequently happens, the point of transition between the trans-parent and the solid method is the point at which we find some of the most perfect works of art ; so it is in the early pictures of Titian, and the later pictures of Rubens, that the balance between gem-like brilliancy and pearly coolness of colour, between delicacy and breadth, between decorative splendour and harmony with natural appearances, is most consummately pre served.

The capacities of more solid methods of painting proved various enough to occupy all the chief masters of the seventeenth and eighteenth centuries, and it was only in England, in the hands of Gainsborough, that the Flemish technique was for a moment revived. In some of Gainsborough's later landscapes, such as *The Market Cart* in the National Gallery, and to a less degree in some of his portraits, we again meet with thin transparent painting that depends almost wholly for its effect upon the luminous ground underneath it. Here we find the transparency allied with a looseness and freedom of brushwork comparable to that of Rubens, and to new splendours of glowing colour.

Then in the early first half of the nineteenth century we find another great English colourist, Turner, gradually discarding the solid method of his youth, and painting thinly, upon canvases loaded with a prepara-'ion of thick flake white, those marvellous visions which have had such a profound influence upon the tone and feeling of modern landscape. The series of Turner's studies in the Tate Gallery is enough, by itself, to indicate that the transparent method, with hardly any essential modification from the Flemish practice, may, when skilfully used, render effects of light and colour and atmosphere as brilliantly as the most forcible and scientific Impressionism, retaining all the while all that suavity of handling and texture which counts for so much in decorative effect, but which solid painting has to forego.

The early work of the Pre-raphaelites points the same moral. Here, as we learn from Mr. Holman Hunt, the canvas was covered with a thin coat of flake white mixed with a very little varnish, and on this luminous foundation, before it was thoroughly dry, the colour was applied thinly and lightly, each part being finished completely at one sitting. The result was a force and luminosity of colouring which, even now, make the Pre-raphaelite pictures more powerful than anything except the works of the primitive masters, and at the time of their first exhibition may have been responsible for some of the hostility they aroused. Of this brilliancy Millais's *Ophelia* in the Tate Gallery is a characteristic specimen: it could hang without discredit by the side of a fine Memling.

Lastly, among living painters, reference must be made to the work of Mr. Orchardson. Here the ground appears less luminous, the colour scheme more cautious and sober, than was the case with Turner or the Pre-raphaelites; but once more we find a peculiar harmonious warmth and a pleasant lightness of touch bestowing refinement and distinction on work which intrinsically might be thought somewhat deficient in power.

Although the record of transparent oil painting since the sixteenth century has been thus fragmentary and spasmodic, it is none the less remarkable. On examination, too, it is clear that its abandonment, first in Italy and afterwards in Northern Europe, was due to temporary, local or accidental causes.

The early Flemish masters proved that it was eminently suitable for a delicate, if somewhat static, form of portraiture, and for the realistic painting of interiors. Their success in this latter field was repeated by Teniers and Brouwer, while the work of Van Ostade and often of De Hooch, is executed upon practically the same principle. Rubens proved that with but few modifications it was capable of rendering landscape, portraits and the nude figure with a freedom which the earlier masters lacked, and the results he obtained were confirmed by Gainsborough, Turner, and the youthful Millais.

On considering this record three prominent facts stand out:

(1) The most perfect paintings produced by this method are easel pictures of moderate size.

Exceptions will at once occur to the mind, notably the large triptych by Hugo van der Goes, which is now among the treasures of the Uffizi, and certain works by

Rubens and Gainsborough. The first-named painting, however, is really in the nature of a marvellous " tour de force." As a picture pure and simple it is too minute for its scale, and with all its perfection looks over-crowded. The larger works of Rubens are just those in which his departure from the purely transparent treatment is most marked—where he obtains his effects only by using opaque colour much more freely than when working on panels or on small canvases.

The charge of flimsiness is sometimes brought against the art of Gainsborough, when he is pitted against other great masters, and it is just when he works in transparent colour on a large scale that the charge comes within the bounds of reason. With him, as with Rubens, the transparent method shows to the best advantage in paintings of moderate size, and on that scale a very considerable freedom of brushwork is admissible. In quite small panels the more precise treatment appears to be advantageous, though by no means necessary.

(2) Without exception the paintings produced by the transparent method are brilliant in colour, and have retained this brilliancy with little or no loss for more than four centuries.

The fact is the more remarkable because this excel-lence of colour is not confined to the great masters, but is inherited by even their humblest scholars and followers. The primitive painters of the Netherlands,

Germany, and France, are alike in this respect. Even with artists who are otherwise clumsy and incompetent we invariably find rich and glowing colour, though in some cases, notably in Germany, it may incline towards violence, and in others may verge upon a brownish monochrome.

Since the transparent method makes even the most sober pigment take on a luminous and gem-like quality, it would seem specially applicable to subjects where the colouring has of necessity to be somewhat quiet. It is a common experience that the use of quiet colours in solid painting leads to heaviness or dulness; with transparent painting this danger might be avoided.

Whatever therefore the advantages of transparent oil painting to a great colourist, it is evidently a process of inestimable value to those whose feeling for colour is imperfect or undeveloped. This much at least is certain; in no other form of the graphic arts has harmonious colouring been produced so consistently; nor has any process of painting hitherto discovered by the wit of man given promise of greater permanence.

At first sight it would seem as if a solid body of strong pigment would be sure to outlast a thin coat. In practice just the reverse holds true. To make the solid pigment really manageable it has to be mixed with a considerable proportion of oil. This oil in the course of time forms a yellow film on the surface of the picture, so that all solidly painted works tend in time to get darker and warmer in tone. If other vehicles are used, the results may be still more disastrous, as the case of Reynolds shows: while the risk of the colours acting chemically upon each other is naturally augmented with each addition to the complexity of the processes employed. The early Dutch and Flemish paintings have already outlasted the vast majority of their successors, and bid fair to shine with undiminished lustre when the bulk of the pictures produced to-day have become heavy and dull.

Moreover, the smooth surface of a thinly painted picture is no inconsiderable help towards the preservation of the colours in their unsullied purity, especially at a stage of civilisation when pictures have frequently to be kept in dusty, smoky cities. On a smooth surface dirt finds no hold; but, if it once gets into the crevices of a roughly painted picture, it is practically irremovable, and cannot fail in time to become a serious blemish.

(3) The transparent method admits of little or no correction.

Hence it can only be employed by a painter who knows exactly what he wants to do, and has the skill to do it at once. If the painter changes his mind and tries to alter his design by repainting, the very act of repainting involves the destruction of the transparency of colour on which the method depends. So we find even very great artists like Van Eyck, Holbein and Rubens beginning with a carefully planned design, upon which the colours can be laid once for all with absolute certainty. The Pre-raphaelites did the same, while the far less rigidly compact designs of Gainsborough seem to have been made out with some completeness in black and white before a start was made with the colouring. Turner alone seems to have come near to improvising but, even in his case, the position of the principal lights was first fixed by a forcible impasto of white paint.

The amount of previous preparation required will naturally vary with the aims and powers of the artist. Where extreme accuracy of form is required as in portraiture or figure work even the most gifted painter will hardly be able to dispense with a careful drawing to guide his eye. The less his power and knowledge, the more detailed will that underlaying preparation have to be, so that little or nothing may be left to chance. With many forms of landscape a greater freedom would be admissible, but any one who experiments in the process will be wise to err on the side of caution, and to make very sure of what he is going to do before starting work, since to correct or alter is to lose transparency, and therewith the *raison d'être* of the process.

At a time when the easel picture of small or moderate size is the form of painting for which

there is the most general demand, an attempt to
revive the method of the early Flemish masters
might be worth serious consideration. It is more
exacting than work in solid pigment, and is more
limited perhaps in its powers of representation; but
its possibilities, especially in the matter of colour, are
great enough to outweigh far heavier disadvantages.
No process known to the graphic arts tends so
directly towards unity of colouring; none appears
capable of greater vitality and freshness of effect;
while the modest scale which suits it best should
prevent this vitality from becoming unrestful. It is
capable of infinitely delicate gradation; yet, in this
respect, it must admit some inferiority to processes
which suggest the variety of substance and texture
which we find in the mature works of Titian or
Rembrandt. Gainsborough, however, has proved it as
capable of tenderness as Rubens proved it capable
of strength, and Holbein of noble precision, so that
its limitations may, after all, be more apparent than
real.

CHAPTER XV

OIL PAINTING : THE MIXED METHOD

WHAT I have termed the mixed method of oil painting, depending in part upon the effect of transparent or translucent pigment upon a light ground, and in part upon the use of opaque pigment, is the process of oil painting most commonly employed by the old masters. The proportions of transparent and opaque elements may vary very considerably. Sometimes the transparent element preponderates so much as to approach the Flemish method closely. At others the pigment may be of such thickness and substance as to approach the border line of universal opacity.

Between these extremes we shall find the mature work of Titian, Tintoret, and Veronese ; of Rembrandt, Van Dyck, Hals, and most of the Dutch masters of genre ; of Velasquez and Goya, and Whistler ; of Reynolds, Hogarth, Wilson, Crome, Constable and the youthful Turner ; of Daumier and Delacroix ; of Millet, and the painters of Barbizon, in fact of almost every painter from the latter part of the sixteenth

century to the latter half of the nineteenth. Historically
the process is an extension of transparent oil painting,
and our study of it must begin with Titian, upon
whose practice the style, not only of his Italian
successors, but also that of the chief painters of
Spain, France, and Northern Europe, for some
three centuries, is really founded.

The accounts which have come down to us of
Titian's method of work are not quite clear (the
writers appear to have confused his earlier and later
manners), but it is not impossible, by reading them
in connection with his paintings, to recognise the
essential features of his system. In his earlier works
the whole subject seems first to have been carried
out, with some completeness, in transparent brown
upon a luminous ground. This first painting seems
to have been in tempera, and the ground a white
ground like those used for tempera. This monochrome foundation was left to dry thoroughly; then
the oil colours were applied, sometimes transparent
and sometimes opaque, as the occasion demanded,
the tints being frequently softened, spread and blended
with the fingers. It would seem that the first colouring was done in broad, flat, map-like masses. The
work was then put aside for some considerable time,
all excess of oil being bleached out by exposure
to sunshine. Then the final painting was begun,
with scumbles of opaque colour and glazes of trans-

parent colour, each coat being thoroughly dried before the application of the next.

This process produced what are perhaps the most beautiful oil paintings in the world, of which the *Bacchus and Ariadne*, in the National Gallery, will serve as an example. Two points in connection with it deserve to be noticed. In the first place the transparent brown underpainting was never covered over in the shadows, and opaque pigment, when used at all, was used in thin translucent films. Hence Titian's youthful works retain much of the gem-like beauty of colour that is found in Flemish art, and in his early manhood this quality is still retained; though it is modified in an ever-increasing degree by the cool pearly tones resulting from the rather more generous use of opaque pigment.

Secondly, the perfect drying of each film before the application of the next removed all superfluous oil. Titian's earlier works, in consequence, have retained their brilliancy just as well as the pictures of the early Flemish masters have done, although the amount of oil required was considerable enough to have proved a serious danger, had it not been removed by exposure to sunshine.

In later years Titian discarded this method. Into the reasons of the change we need not inquire. Probably the necessity of getting through the mass of commissions with which he was honoured, possibly too the desire of adding certain new qualities to the art of painting which increased experience prompted, led him to adopt another system of work.

He now took to making his first painting in solid colour, possibly black, white, and red. This preparation was of some thickness both in the lights and in the shadows. It was carried to such a degree of finish that it was practically a monochrome version of the picture, and was kept in rather a high key. When this preliminary painting was finished and accurate in all its parts, it was dried as before, and then the colours were added by glazing. In the hands of such a great master the method produced noble results ; the glazes upon the solid under-paint providing effects of rich, broken colour well adapted to the uncertain vibrant illumination in which Titian's latest subjects are viewed.

Yet, in clearness, freshness, and brilliancy, these works of Titian's old age are undeniably inferior to those of his youth, and their sombre grandeur is only now and then (as in the superb *Pietà* in the Accademia) a perfect compensation for the vanished brightness. The solid underpainting, even if it were kept very pale, was infinitely less luminous than the older grounds of white gesso, and so reflected much less light through the transparent colour subsequently laid upon it. In practice, it will be found exceedingly difficult to keep this under-painting quite pale. A certain amount of force is needed to separate one tone from another, yet every increase in force of tone implies a corresponding loss of brilliancy in the finished work.

What was a difficulty for Titian was a catastrophe for his successors. Being a great draughtsman, he could represent solid forms by delicate gradations of modelling; they had to represent them by excess of projection. He could, so to speak, model perfectly in low relief; they had to use high relief. He could finish his solid foundation with one or two paintings, and his glazings with one or two more; they arrived at completeness only after many reworkings. Titian's pictures in consequence were painted with comparatively little oil; his successors used a great deal of it. He was careful to dry his pictures thoroughly between every stage; they frequently seem to have neglected this precaution. Titian's work in consequence has usually kept its tone fairly well; the paintings of his successors are commonly too black in the shadows and too yellow in the lighter parts.

By tracing this difference in some detail, we can see clearly why all oil painting which depends upon an elaborate succession of processes, is liable to be rather dark at the outset, and to grow darker still with time. Even if the original be in a somewhat light key from the start, the danger is not entirely removed; for the quantity of oil suspended in the substance of the paint will tend, in time, to make the half-tones dull and the pale tones yellow.

Thus it is that the paintings of the seventeenth and eighteenth centuries which have best stood the test of time are generally those which were painted most swiftly, and upon a light ground. A ground of middle tint is convenient for securing unity of tone, and has been the fashion with more than one school and period: but heaviness and darkness have generally resulted, notably in the case of those who worked on the grounds of strong red which at one time seem to have been in common use.

Yet a strong red ground may sometimes be serviceable. Constable, for many of his paintings, and for the majority of his sketches, employed a foundation of strong reddish-brown. In his case it served both as a connecting link between the detached touches by which his studies were built up, and as a contrast to the cool greens and blues and grays that he favoured, which might otherwise have looked cold. It must be remembered, too, that Constable generally painted with a full brush, so that his pigment was thick enough to prevent the dark foundation from lowering the tones materially. In one of his early experiments on a large scale, the famous *White Horse*, he did use thin pigment over a strong warm ground, with the result that the picture has lost its first brightness.

Among subsequent artists, Whistler may be men-

tioned as one who has suffered materially from the
same cause. Being attracted by the delightful effect
which blue or gray produce when spread thinly upon
a dark ground, Whistler frequently used them in this
way, with the result that some of his most delightful
paintings are darkening steadily year by year, as the
ground begins to tell more and more through the delicate films of paint laid over it.

Though Van Dyck learned many of the secrets of
his art from the example of Titian and the great Venetians, during the years which he spent in Italy, he
could never forget what he had learned in youth from
Rubens. His method is a dexterous blend of the
transparent painting of Northern Europe with the richness and variety of quality characteristic of the South,
much of his work being based upon a foundation of
monochrome, usually cool and silvery compared with
the glowing monochrome of Rubens, light and spark-
ling compared with the preparatory work of the Italians.
With his practice that of many of the best Dutch
masters may be classed, Rembrandt and Hals being
two remarkable exceptions.

Rembrandt's practice varies greatly at different
periods of his life, but in its most characteristic phase
it resembles the practice of Rubens far more nearly
than a casual inspection might suggest. Instead, however, of leaving the surface of the canvas to serve as a
ground for all but the highest lights, as Rubens did

Rembrandt first worked out a monochrome sketch in a fiercely modelled impasto containing much solid white. Upon this impasto, when it had dried thoroughly, he appears to have painted his picture, largely in transparent colour, but using opaque colour freely whenever the effect required it. Even the high lights were glazed, and the shadows being painted with rich dark tones, brought his works into a golden harmony, to which any slight yellowing caused by the oily vehicle employed could do no very serious damage.

Velasquez and Hals solved the problem in another way; perhaps accidentally. By painting *alla prima*, or nearly so, upon light-coloured canvas, they succeeded in freeing themselves to a great extent from the difficulty which attends more elaborate processes of oil painting. One coat of paint, applied thinly and swiftly, may contain a good deal of oil, but the chances are it will contain much less than a picture that is built up by successive stages and repeated glazings, each preceded perhaps by "oiling up." The method of Velasquez is not so uniformly direct as that of Hals, but both agree in approximating to consummately skilful sketching, and are therefore hailed as the pioneers of the direct painting which is the fashion at the present day.

I have pointed out elsewhere * that the method of Hals attains its swiftness and spirit by the sacrifice of realism of colour. In the slightly less direct method

* *Burlington Magazine,* January 1908, vol. xii. pp. 202–205.

of Velasquez the colours of nature are matched much more truly; indeed his fame rests on the fact that no one has combined such decision and finality of brush-work with so much naturalism and pictorial good taste Something of these qualities survives in his country-man Goya, through whom Velasquez comes into touch with Whistler and Manet. In the latter we meet with attempts to surprise more garish effects of daylight, and a less dignified humanity, which prepare the way (*viâ* Carolus Duran) for Sargent.

In England, the moment the English became painters at all, the value of this direct painting was discovered by Hogarth. His finished pictures are not always completely satisfactory, but his rare oil sketches are among the most perfect products of the English or of any other school. As with Hals and Velasquez, the colour-scheme is modest. The ground is usually a warm gray, upon which Hogarth's touches of white and lilac, and rose pink and dull green, tell with exquisite freshness. Had it not been for the coming of Reynolds a new art might possibly have risen from these begin-nings, for which a certain daintiness of touch and sober freshness of colour in one or two of Hogarth's forgotten contemporaries seem to be preparing the way.

Nor can the achievement of Wilson be overlooked. Wilson was originally fired by the example of the degenerate heirs of a Venetian tradition; not the elaborate tradition of Titian, but a later and more direct realism, retaining however something of the old Venetian feeling for colour, which in landscape was represented first by Canaletto, then by the more flimsy yet enchanting Guardi. With Guardi, indeed, Wilson has more in common than with his immediate teachers, Zuccarelli and Vernet, both in his breadth of design and in his feeling for colour.

Wilson's pictures seem almost always to have been painted directly, but he used large quantities of linseed oil as a diluent. In his Italian pictures, as already mentioned, this was usually dried out by the climate; in his English pictures it has too often remained, to the serious detriment of the tone and colour.

The practice of Reynolds put an end, for the time being, to all these direct methods, so far at least as figure-painting was concerned. Though the names of Michelangelo and Raphael dominate his " Discourses," and though his notes show his interest in the great Venetians and in Rubens, his paintings indicate a student of Rembrandt and a worshipper of Correggio. Under the inexhaustible variety of his poses, of his schemes of lighting and of his patterns of colour, these two influences survive. Yet neither the profound concentration of Rembrandt nor the pearly flesh tones of Correggio were enough for Reynolds. To Rembrandt's mystery of shadow he wished to add a Venetian splendour of colour, to Correggio's silvery light he wished to add a richness of substance previously unknown to oil painting. To solve the first problem he indulged in repeated experiments in glazing with almost every vehicle, safe or unsafe, that is known to the painter's art; to solve the second he resorted to equally dangerous experiments in pictorial cookery.

The result was not so wholly disastrous as his critics have sometimes made out. Many of his pictures certainly are mere ghosts of their former selves; few, and those not always his most interesting works, have stood the ordeal of time without some marked deterioration. Yet occasionally Reynolds did get very near to both his ideals, and even where the dangerous methods he employed have produced their natural result, and left us hardly more than a shadow of some once glowing canvas, the shadow is still more attractive than the successes of his pupils and followers. Indeed we may sometimes suspect that Reynolds did not wholly dislike the pleasant variety of texture, which a moderate *craquelure* provides.

However, quite apart from the asphaltum with which he sometimes enriched his shadows, and the wax with which he softened and "fattened" his lights, the mere practice of depending for effect upon successive paintings with very liquid colour was, in itself, enough to ensure the ultimate darkening of the shadows. Yet the beauty of Sir Joshua's results blinded his contemporaries to this radical defect, and painting in England for some thirty years was practically buried underneath the "brown sauce," to which his example led the way. We see it even in the early work of Watts; it darkens much of the best work of Wilkie, but its effect on landscape was still more fatal, and therefore, perhaps, led the more rapidly to a reaction in that province.

Crome, the head of the Norwich School, had the good fortune to receive only the training of a house, coach and sign painter. His early work is thus often as broad and direct as that of Velasquez. The influences of Wilson, Gainsborough, and Hobbema make themselves felt in later years, and his methods become elaborate; but Crome's certainty of hand enabled him to obtain his effects so swiftly, that his most highly finished works retain much of the quality of direct painting.

Cotman is no less masterly in his use of oil paint, sometimes approaching Crome in tonality, but more usually preferring a much bolder range of colour, in which strong blues play a prominent part. Were his paintings in oil less rare they would be more generally studied, for in their austere reliance upon definite pattern they stand almost alone in English art.

Coming next to Turner and Constable, we find that Turner's youthful works are elaborately executed with much glazing. In his middle period the ground becomes lighter and the pigment thinner, till at last his desire for brightness compels him practically to become a worker on the Flemish method, though he uses it with a freedom and daring of which even Rubens never dreamed. His earlier works, originally full of strong contrasts, have darkened considerably owing to the elaboration of their technique, so that such things as the *Calais Pier*, with all their power, are too heavy to be pleasant decoration. After a time Turner gradually discovered that much of the fault lay with the ground and, by working on a foundation of thick flake white, he was enabled to use even opaque colour without losing luminosity. As time goes on the loading of the ground becomes heavier and heavier, while the superposed colours become thinner and thinner, till his method at last becomes a transparent one.

Constable also began with elaborate methods and repeated glazings, and employed them in his pictures right up to his thirty-fifth year. His sketches from nature however almost from the first were painted directly, without retouching, and vary from his youth to his old age only in the thickness of their pigment, and the freedom of their handling. After a while he learned to build up large pictures on a brown foundation of the traditional kind, not hesitating to employ glazing where necessary, but minimising its tendency to darken by taking care that the body of light pigment beneath was considerable, and often working into the glaze itself with cool opaque colour. In his later years, desiring still greater force and brightness, he used the palette knife to apply touches and scrapings of pure colour, and so became a pioneer of modern solid painting; although, as he retained the brown monochrome sketch as the foundation of his design, his principle was really more allied to the Old Masters than to the Impressionists.

In France the primitive Flemish tradition was replaced in the sixteenth century by the Italian style. Then the influence of Rubens was felt, and these two traditions dominate most French work up to the nineteenth century. Poussin may stand as the great representative of the Italian Renaissance, Watteau as the heir of the Flemish one. Chardin used the full resources of both transparent and opaque colour with consummate artistic power. but it will be noticed that, while some of his most directly painted pictures have lasted perfectly, those where the workmanship is more elaborate, and the pigment heavily loaded and glazed, have cracked and darkened. The swift brushwork of Fragonard has on the whole lasted much better.

The pioneers of the Romantic movement in the nineteenth century, Gros and Gericault, retained so much of the oily elaborate manner that their pictures are now almost uniformly brown and dark. Delacroix had the advantage of seeing Constable's work, and this taught him to aim at brightness; but he sought for it rather by painting his lights thickly, than by giving attention to the luminosity of his ground. Hence, though most of his work is directly and forcibly painted, the shadows have become heavy. Both Daumier and Millet often suffer from the same cause, the darkening in the case of Millet being often augmented by the frequency with which he re-worked his canvases.

Theodore Rousseau's practice in landscape was not dissimilar from that of Millet, and his work generally appears to us now in a more sombre guise than it did to his contemporaries. Corot's method has lasted better. At first he painted entirely in solid paint. Then shaking off the dryness of his early manner, he gradually advanced to a lighter style. Upon a luminous white foundation he appears to have built up his picture in transparent monochrome. When this was dry, colours were applied in thin films, forcible impasto being reserved for the high lights.

Lastly a word may be said of Monticelli, Courbet, and Manet, through whom we come to the Impressionists. In the best works of Monticelli we find glazes of the richest colours applied over luminous white, and then retouched with opaque colour in considerable body. The effect is striking in a somewhat incoherent way, and where the ground has been strong enough his pictures have stood well. Courbet's methods vary much, being sometimes dependent upon very thick opaque pigment, modified at the last by a glaze, at others being thin and direct. Had his grounds been brighter these last would have been more uniformly well preserved; the former class remain powerful but rather heavy in effect. The direct painting favoured by Manet in his earlier period has darkened a little, perhaps, but otherwise remains unaltered. His paint seems to have contained no more oil than was needed to make it manageable. *Mutatis mutandis* his method might be compared with that of Sargent, though his colour-schemes, being much more deliberate, should suffer less from the slight dulling and "leatheriness" which come with time than Sargent's complicated naturalism may do.

I have sketched the progress of the mixed method of oil painting at some length, because it is the method employed by the great majority of working artists. There are good reasons for its popularity. It is capable of the utmost variety of expression: permitting the plastic suggestiveness and luminous force of a solid impasto to be combined with the richness of thin, liquid and transparent colour. The works of Rembrandt and Reynolds exhibit many illustrations of the felicitous blending of these extremes. Indeed, it seems at first sight to possess the advantages of both the opaque and transparent methods, without their disadvantages; and the long roll of the great artists who have employed it, is sufficient testimony to its practical convenience.

Not only does it possess variety of substance and

texture, but much of this variety can be obtained at a single sitting. The use of thin liquid pigment enables the artist to spread his shadows broadly and rapidly: while the lighter portions of the subject can be suggested with equal ease by the use of forcible impasto. It is thus almost perfectly adapted for making sketches and studies.

For elaborate painting too it offers many advantages. The design can be first sketched in ; then any number of subsequent paintings can be executed upon it; the most elaborate effects of quality can be attained by judicious use of glazing and scumbling ; unsatisfactory passages can be altered; the technique of a picture may in fact be made just as simple or complex as the painter chooses. If he be sure of himself, and his subject is one which is best treated by direct painting, he can be direct ; if it calls for extreme subtlety of modelling or colour, as in the case of certain kinds of figure and landscape painting, he can refine *ad infinitum* upon his first conception.

Yet, in considering its record as a whole, one unpleasant fact has to be reckoned with. A very large proportion of the pictures thus painted fall short of complete success ; more still are to some extent lacking in decorative beauty. In the case of transparent oil painting, and of tempera too, the feebler men produce pictures that have some outward attractiveness of general colour. Their pictures may be ill-conceived, ill-drawn, and tamely painted, yet they make excellent decoration.

In the case of the mixed method, it is hardly an exaggeration to say that the only pleasant pictures made by its help have been made by great masters. All other men, clever and dull, proficient and incompetent alike, have produced pictures which are rarely pleasant in colour, and are usually heavy in tone. If we pause for a moment to recall the thousands and thousands of dark and disagreeable canvases for which the method is responsible, we may begin to see that, while it has been of service to a number of great artists, it has been the reverse of helpful to nearly all who have fallen short of supreme excellence. Their failure is accompanied with a colouring that is either too cold or too heavy, and with a tone that is dull and dead, the latter fault being practically universal.

The cause of this failure may not be apparent at first sight, but a little consideration gives us two or three facts to work upon. In the first place we often find sketches and slight studies which have retained their freshness, while the finished pictures of the very same artists are uniformly dark and heavy. Secondly the artists who have used the method with success, have either approximated in their practice to the transparent method, by painting lightly over a luminous ground; or have painted *alla prima* so that their pictures have the quality of very brilliant

P

sketches. Van Dyck and Hals, Velasquez and Goya, Watteau and the Barbizon painters, Turner and Crome, might be instanced as examples of the former practice; the paintings of Tiepolo and Canaletto, of Guardi and Whistler, and the oil sketches of Constable as examples of the latter.

Again, those who have made copies of the work of the old masters will have noticed that, after a time, the copies usually become heavier, browner, and duller than the originals; especially where the painting process has been elaborate, and has necessitated the use of much oil, or has been used upon a dark ground. So constant is this change, that it is usually possible to distinguish at once between an original painting and a copy simply by the difference of the tone; the original being always the fresher in effect of the two.

It is generally recognised by painters that this darkening is due to the action of the oil mixed with the pigments, and the fear of it has driven many moderns who paint in a high key to use their colours as dry as possible, and in considerable body, so that the risk of future change may be minimised.

Oil, as already indicated more than once, tends, after a time, to rise to the surface of a picture and settle there in the form of a yellowish film.* The more oil

---

* I have throughout used oil as meaning linseed, poppy- or nut-oil These were the oils commonly used by the old masters, and the best prepared colours at the present day are generally ground

the picture contains the thicker this film will be, and the greater the subsequent lowering of the tone.

Even a picture painted *alla prima* may suffer seriously from this cause if it be painted either with too much medium, or with too great a body of solid colour. The case of Richard Wilson has already been mentioned in this connection. Thick, solid paint as it comes from the tube may not alter very much, but the amount of oil contained in ordinary tube colours is so large that, if they are used in any considerable body, enough oil will ultimately come to the surface to dull all the more delicate tones. The painters who, like Guardi or Constable, have worked on reddish grounds, have thus to sail constantly between the Scylla of painting too thin, in which case the ground will show through in the course of time (as Whistler's dark grounds have done), and the Charybdis of painting too thickly, and thereby deadening their colour.

On the whole it is evident that a firm white ground, if necessary veiled with some simple tint, is the first condition of safety in this form of oil painting. Next, the painting should be as thin as possible; if done *alla prima*, so much the better. If subsequent paintings

in linseed oil. Thus, although a painter may mix his colours with varnish or petroleum or turpentine to get particular effects, or to secure ease in manipulation, his pigment will contain a large amount of oil—nay, even if he dispenses with all diluents, and dries his tube colours on blotting-paper before applying them much oil will still be left.

and repaintings are necessary, each should be thoroughly dried and bleached before the next one is started. Except on these conditions, the mixed method of oil painting cannot be regarded as likely to retain its 'reshness.

The brushes used by painters have so direct an influence upon their work as to deserve a few words of notice. Very large brushes suggest breadth but may lead to vacuity: very small brushes suggest finish but may lead to feebleness. This last defect is the one most feared by the painters of to-day, so the brushes they use are neither very small nor very soft. Yet exclusive devotion to middle-sized brushes has disadvantages of its own. In the first place it tends to produce monotony of touch, a failing pardonable in a large mural decoration but tiresome in the case of small pictures where the brushwork is clearly seen. Again, and this is more serious, it makes real delicacy of handling impossible, and thereby sins against the condition of infinity, as it sins against the condition of vitality by its monotonous character. Logic would thus seem to advise the employment of large brushes for laying in the masses of a picture, and of small brushes to complete the details, these last having points fine enough for the most precise drawing where precision is needed. The use of softer brushes than the ordinary hog tools for passages of special delicacy is also suggested.

CHAPTER XVI

OIL PAINTING: THE OPAQUE METHOD

To dispense entirely with the light reflected from a luminous ground by working in thick opaque pigment is a practice essentially modern. Earlier painters had often worked thickly, but this thick painting had only been a preparation for subsequent glazes of transparent colour which made the real picture. In the modern process there is no glazing, and the effect is obtained by the light reflected from fresh masses of solid colour. The process is a popular one, especially on the Continent, and has the backing of the impressionists, and of two great modern masters, Watts and Puvis de Chavannes.

Let us see first of all how far the method accords with our four pictorial conditions. To Unity it is obviously favourable. The matt surface of the solid paint has fewer variations of texture and quality, and is less likely to be broken up by extreme contrasts of tone, than that of canvases where liquid and solid pigment are used side by side. For the same reason we may assume that the condition of Repose can

229

also be easily fulfilled on the opaque system, although the liberal use of primary colours by its modern exponents might lead us to think otherwise. But the very qualities which make unity and repose come so naturally, are adverse when Vitality and Infinity have to be considered. The solid matt surface of the paint is as opposed to the one as its comparative intractability, owing to the absence of a diluent, is opposed to the other.

The men who have used the opaque method with success have overcome these difficulties in different ways. The Impressionists, as a group, neutralise the natural density and heaviness of their pigment by a combination of devices, which in their day were new to art but which have now become common property. In the first place they aim at compensating for want of vitality in pigment, by exceptional vitality in colour, handling, and design. They use only primary colours; and they avoid dulling their brightness by any mixing. When a compound tone is needed, the artist mentally resolves it into its primary constituents, and applies small touches of those pure primaries side by side on his canvas, till this mosaic or patchwork matches the tint he requires. With this brilliant vibrant method of applying his colour there is allied, in good Impressionist pictures, a capricious vigour of design, suggested no doubt by Japanese art. And the combination is certainly never devoid of vitality. Where it does fail is in the matter of infinity.

Even with its most skilled and gifted practitioners the method can never be more than a somewhat rough and ready process—spirited, luminous and vibrant perhaps, but lacking in those refinements and subtleties to which other methods of painting owe so large a part of their charm. I think it is for this reason that we find Impressionist painting just a little empty, and lacking that richness of content which is so considerable an element in the pleasure we take in any picture. The great Impressionists, it is true, seem to have recognised this danger, and have worked on a scale so modest that the peril is minimised; but their followers have been less wise. They have attempted to paint large canvases on principles which, as we have seen, are applicable only to small ones, with the result that no violent forcing of the colour or the design is enough to counterbalance the deadly monotony of raw pigment and uniform spotty handling, displayed on a surface several square feet (or yards) in extent.

Of all the forms of painting which the world has hitherto seen I know of none more wholly intolerable. The sugared illustrations of once popular Academicians may long be appreciated on the walls of a nursery; the religious and heroic paintings of the seventeenth and eighteenth centuries may long decorate the dark corners of a stair or a private chapel; but this particular development of Impressionism seems to serve no conceivable use, as it conveys no reasonable pleasure, and I think time will consign it to that remote and mysterious exile in which the academic art of early-Victorian Germany has been buried out of sight.

The qualities of unity and repose, which it naturally possesses, render the opaque method particularly suitable for decorative painting, and it is therefore hardly strange that its greatest achievement hitherto should have been in decorative work. The large mural pictures of Puvis de Chavannes are perhaps the most notable specimens of their class since the day of Tiepolo, and now that fresco has repeatedly proved its inability to withstand the cold and damp of a northern climate, his practice will probably be followed in future as the most perfect available substitute.

We have seen how the natural difficulties of the method are want of vitality and of infinity : how the Impressionists conquered the first difficulty but not always the second ; and how their followers have come to almost complete disaster when attempting to work on any but a small scale. Puvis de Chavannes succeeded in conquering both difficulties, and that when painting on an immense scale.

To obtain vitality the Impressionists forced their colour to the most brilliant pitch which could be obtained with paint. This device was endurable enough in a panel one or two feet square, but for a large mural painting it was out of the question. In two early works at Amiens, more especially in the *War*, Puvis de

Chavannes proved that he could obtain vitality when he
chose to do so by force of colour, but the result there
achieved did not satisfy him. In his opinion decorative
work needed even more repose than those stately
paintings possess. So his later decorations are all conceived in the palest possible key, where such oppositions of colour as do occur cannot ever be very strong
or sensational.

Hence the master relies for vitality almost wholly
upon the planning of his subject, and upon the robust
contours of the Arcadian humanity with which his
canvases are so largely occupied. The movement of
these massive figures, even when it is most stately and
slow, is suggestive of huge physical strength held in
reserve; the full supple forms of the women and
children exhale a sense of the same full-blooded well-
being, the same impregnable health. This spirit of re-
strained power breathes from the landscape also ; from
the massive rocks tufted here and there with sprays of
herbage, from the sweep of the low hills to some quie
French water side, or from the poplar shafts that rise
like pillars against the winter sky. The stimulus is
heightened by the exquisite use made of silhouette.
Where one broad restful mass meets its neighbour, we
find the drawing of the edges alive with exquisite
detail, so that the sharp fresh contour of a flower
or a cluster of leaves as it cuts against the sky,
seems to acquire a new virtue by the strangeness of its

appearance in a world where all else is so large and massive.

A certain unexpectedness, too, in the very planning of these great works constantly stimulates and perplexes the mind. In this compositional subtlety, this knowledge which disdains all the recognised tricks of design, we have not only a proof of the painter's creative originality, but also one of the means by which he gets the utmost value out of his materials, and produces a complex elusive whole out of elements ostensibly simple and austere. The colours which he affects, faint gray and lilac, cool green, cool brown and fresh pallid white, have the same strangeness, the same elusiveness; indeed, the more we study the work of Puvis de Chavannes, the more shall we be impressed with the richness of content and the noble liveliness which underlie his seeming coldness, restraint, and abstraction. No mural decoration for large buildings has ever observed the conditions proper to such work with more complete success; and the style and method invented by him cannot fail to be followed and, perhaps (if another great genius is born), developed still further, wherever intelligent persons desire public buildings to be intelligently adorned.

Of Watts we may speak more briefly. His use of opaque colour dates from the latter part of his life, and was preceded by long years of reliance upon traditional methods. It is said to have been adopted from his desire to avoid the darkening caused by the use of too much oil, and not with any view of making a radical change in handling, or to produce some novel effect, as was the method used by the Impressionists. Nor does it resemble the deliberate laying of one thick even tone by the side of another by which Puvis de Chavannes constructed his pictures. It is based rather on the regular method of oil painting, except in so far as the pigment is applied almost dry instead of in a semi-liquid state, shadows and mixed tones being obtained by crumbling one colour over another instead of by liquid glazes.

The paintings produced by this method rank among the finest products of the English school. Often they have obvious faults; but they possess also the rarest virtues. The sense of original design is intermittent, many pictures recalling faintly the standard compositions of earlier times, while others rank in originality with those of Puvis de Chavannes, and they could have no higher praise. The ideals are always noble, though here and there they are overcharged with sentiment. The colour is rich and superb, yet with all its splendour is often reminiscent of the great Venetians rather than actually inventive. Yet the balance and fusion of fine qualities in the best work of Watts is so complete that we need not ask whether the creative element in his genius was really so great as with some other famous painters. His best pictures can hang with credit in the loftiest company, and that is the quite conclusive ordeal.

This method of Watts possesses one exceedingly valuable quality. It admits of re-working to an extent impossible in other methods, and though this may sometimes lead to heaviness or fumbling (from which Watts himself does not always escape), it also gives confidence to the hand and mind, thereby encouraging freedom of treatment. It should be specially valuable to those who have to paint easel pictures of consider-able size. Not only does it suit the comparative lightness of tone which we have seen to be specially desirable in the case of large canvases, but the tuning of the whole composition into harmony is made much easier when the process of retouching, or repainting unsatisfactory passages, does not involve the difference of surface or texture which accompanies retouching by the transparent method.

The method is also extraordinarily well suited to a certain kind of portraiture: not the portraiture which calls for a lively sketch, or a flattering piece of mani-pulative dexterity, such as the average society man or society lady expects, but rather that portraiture of the intellect in which Watts holds a place apart from his contemporaries. By a method which permits of con-stant re-working, of the deliberate addition of subtle refinements of modelling to the first broad likeness, a great man's inner mind may be suggested upon canvas with infinitely more chance of success than by methods in which everything depends upon a single coat of paint, however keen the eye and skilful the hand of the master who applies it. The successive films of colour in themselves, too, seem to correspond in some degree to the different phases of the sitter's talent and character, and thus to give a wider and deeper view of him than the most brilliant rendering of his appearance at any single moment.

Of the three methods described, that of Puvis de Chavannes is perfectly suited for mural painting, but not without some modification, in the matter of opacity in the shadows, for easel pictures. In these Puvis himself, while retaining his characteristic methods of design and treatment, worked much more thinly, the colour at times being hardly more than a mere staining of the canvas.

Comparing next the method of Watts with that of the Impressionists, it would seem that the advantage in general lies with the former. It may not reach quite the same pitch of brightness and luminosity; but the slight advantage of the Impressionists in this respect is counter-balanced by more serious defects. Neither method admits of very high finish; but that of Watts allows of far more refinement of modelling and colour, a superiority of great importance in the case of elaborate pictures. It permits also of great variety and freedom of handling, so that the workmanship has never that deadly monotony which causes even the great Impressionists to seem rather tedious when their work is shown in any quantity, and their followers to be positive bores. In point of permanence, too, assuming that each style is carried out with nearly dry pigment, so that the risk of yellowing is reduced to a minimum, the rough granulated surface of much Impressionist work cannot fail in time to be injured far more than the other by the accumulation of dust and dirt in the crevices of the paint. In connection with this matter of dryness, it may be mentioned that Watts, in his fear of ultimate yellowing, extracted occasionally so much of the oil in his pigment that when the picture dried small pieces flaked off.

Owing to the intractability of dry paint, Watts's method would hardly answer for sketching ; nor are large flat tones, such as those which occur in the sky and are needed in decorative work, so readily produced by its aid as by more liquid pigment. These appear to be the worst of its defects, and are trifling compared with its advantages for the making of elaborate easel pictures. Yet painters would be wise, however, to employ it in connection with very firm and vigorous designs ; otherwise the facility with which it admits of re-working may lead to an appearance of fumbling.

PART III

EMPHASIS OF CHARACTER

νικᾷ δ'ὁ πρῶτος καὶ τελευταῖος ὁραμών

CHAPTER XVII

THE PAINTER'S AIMS AND IDEALS

The notion that the culminating glory of painting is a deceptive imitation is still the æsthetic touchstone of the masses; and, modified perhaps by some tags of studio jargon, "sincerity," "values," or the like, it still passes muster in the best society. The slightest acquaintance with what the civilised world has consented to regard as great painting will show this ideal to be false. Had it been true the great painters would be known by their obvious resemblance to nature, and thereby to each other, as one photograph resembles another.

The slightest acquaintance with the history of Art will lead to the same conclusion. The cave men who drew the well-known groups of reindeer, the mammoth, and the terrible cave bear were superb realists, but their realism was as far from being imitation as their scratched bones are from a photographic print. Out of the total mass of visual facts which an animal presented to their eyesight, they abstracted one or two, such as the external contour of the head, trunk and limbs—the place and shape of the eye. These facts the scratch of a sharp stone on some softer surface would perpetuate; and, once so perpetuated, the imagination could easily fill in the colour, the texture of the hide and the minor details. It was needless to do more. The beast was suggested completely.

Here at the very birth of art we find the necessity of selection and omission, with the view to emphatic statement, recognised more generally perhaps than it has ever been recognised since. And with this necessity we may note another characteristic of primitive art—the love of rhythm and pattern. The enjoyment of rhythm for its own sake appears to be an essential factor in the very birth of the art impulse * among savage peoples; and it was only by slow degrees that the pleasant repetition of forms which constitutes a simple pattern developed into more elaborate decorative efforts, involving definite motives derived from natural objects. Rhythm and emphatic vitality may thus be regarded as the dominant qualities in all primitive art.

"Ah!" but the objector may say, "this art was unconscious, savage, infantile, imperfect." Let us then move some stages further in the history of civilisation, when the savage has gathered himself with his neighbours into a tribe, and when tribes have, in course of

* The Origin of the Sense of Beauty. By Felix Clay. London: Smith, Elder, 1908

time, amalgamated into a great state, under the rule of kings or priests to whom the painter is a subject or servant. This is the state of affairs which, in one form or another, existed from the first dawn of civilisation in Egypt and the Eastern Mediterranean, till the decay of the mediæval powers of Europe allowed free citizens to work in free cities.

This great period of art, in which the outbursts of real freedom, as in Greece for example, are local and momentary, may be termed the age of Despotic Art. The artist was then the servant of his rulers. When these were laymen, his business was to celebrate either their personal triumphs or those of their warlike ancestors. When his masters were priests, his business was to celebrate the triumphs of religion. These two branches of Despotic Art, the heroic and the hieratic, have thus a similar foundation. They display also a similar character and a similar technical treatment.

That they may impress the popular imagination both are as imposing in scale as circumstances will allow. Both are plain and straightforward in statement, to catch the popular mind. Both are richly coloured, to delight the popular eye. To make the significance of each figure clear and unmistakable, its contours are marked by strong outlines. To give brightness and force to the colouring, it is applied in flat tints unbroken by shadows. To avoid puzzling the untutored brain, the very designs are reduced to the simplest possible terms.

The figures are as few as will conveniently tell their story; they are surrounded with no more objects than are needed to explain their character; and their predominance is never diminished by a realistic landscape background.

These characteristics are found alike in the temples of Egypt and the palaces of Knossos. For a short time they are threatened by the inquiring Hellenic genius; then, with the decline of the Western Empire, the splendid limitations of mosaic accentuate the Despotic convention, and it lasts unchanged to the very end of the middle ages. It is not till we come to the time of Masaccio and Piero della Francesca that the unearthing of classical sculpture, coupled with personal freedom for the artist, encourage those experiments in the presentation of the human form as something round and substantial, which culminate in Leonardo, Michelangelo, Correggio, and Raphael. If we look to the far East, the prospect will be the same; except that in China the Despotic convention of outline and colour has lasted to our day, while in Japan it has only just now begun to break down under the pressure from Western influences.

It is a common error to speak of Despotic Art as if it were immature, as if its limitations in the matter of shadow and relief were due to ignorance and inexperience. Imperfect it sometimes may be. In Egyptian art the figures might have been less stiffly uniform; in

Crete they sometimes verge upon caricature; in Byzantine work they may assume too much of the rigid character of architecture; with the Italians of the trecento too much of that Byzantine temper may survive; in China forms may be contorted through the connection of painting with calligraphy. Yet with all their defects these various phases of painting serve their destined purpose, and serve it much better than the painting of more sophisticated ages has generally succeeded in doing.

And they succeed in virtue of the things they omit, almost as much as by the assistance of the things they express. Were details more fully realised, we should lose their simple grandeur, their direct mythmical effectiveness; were relief and shadows added, we should lose their breadth and their force of colour; were the figures even more closely imitative of real figures (as some of the Pompeian paintings show), they would cease to have the majesty of legendary heroes, the aloofness of divine or saintly personages—they would bring us into closer contact with earth and the every-day world, until our awe and respect were turned to familiarity.

All heroic and hieratic painting then will have something of this grand and simple character. The contours may be as nobly drawn as human skill can draw them, but they must be firm and definite throughout. The colour may be as brilliant or as quiet as circum stances demand, but it must be applied in masses that are flat or nearly flát. Details, forcible suggestion of relief, and strong shadows must be avoided. In our own day these limitations have been observed and respected only by a single painter, Puvis de Chavannes, but in virtue of that restraint he has taken his place among the great masters.

Any full discussion of this important branch of art lies outside our present scope. Opportunities for its exercise occur with extreme rarity in these days of committees and compromise, although, of all forms of painting, it is incontestably the grandest and noblest. But its characteristics of firm outline and simplicity of treatment have been transferred with marked success to works executed on a smaller scale and in humbler materials. It is to the reminiscence of austere hieratic figure-painting that the great masters of Oriental land-scape (not excepting even the naturalistic Hiroshige), owe their large and restful charm: the prints and drawings of Blake echo, if with somewhat untrained and provincial rudeness, the majestic rhythm of Michelangelo; while, from the frescoes of the earlier Italians, the gem-like water-colours of Rossetti (at least the best of them) derive their stately planning. Though communion with the great masters of mural painting is less openly revealed in the portraits of Reynolds, it underlies none the less their consistent dignity ; indeed its influence upon other branches of

painting has been so universally recognised as bene-
ficial that the painters of all ages but our own have
desired its guidance.

That the result has been pomposity with the vain,
absurdity with the weak, and coldness with the
laborious, is unfortunately too true. Painters have not
always remembered that firmness is perilously near to
rigidity, simplicity to emptiness, and that the one is
most needed where a subject lacks character, the other
where there is too much wealth of material. Used in
their proper place the characteristics of Primitive and
Despotic Art are of inestimable value in ennobling
smaller themes, and if an artist hesitates to employ
them so because they have shipwrecked a hundred of
his predecessors, he should remember that on the
opposite side of the channel yawns the Charybdis of
littleness which has engulfed ten thousand.

With the breaking down of the forms of government
under which heroic and hieratic art most naturally
flourish, we arrive at the more democratic stage of
civilisation in which the painter is a free citizen, at
liberty to work much as his judgment may direct or his
fancy may prompt, subject to personal and local
restrictions. We come, in fact, to the stage of Individual Art. This, so far as painting is concerned, may
be classed under four headings.*

* This classification is in part due to a suggestion made to me by
Mr. Roger Fry, who has already treated the subject with some

(1) Dramatic Painting.   The art of a crisis.

(2) Lyrical Painting.   The art of a mood.

(3) Satiric Painting.   The art of ridicule.

(4) Narrative Painting.   The art of description.

Speaking broadly, all easel pictures may be classed under one or more of these headings.   Now and then it is true we may light upon things with some touch of the heroic and the hieratic ; more frequently, especially in modern times, we find a suggestion of what may be termed Socialist Painting.   Each of these groups of ideas has a separate method of treatment appropriate to it, and may therefore well be separately discussed, although in practice the groups are usually fused and blended, so that the great majority of easel pictures are not exactly typical of any one group, but should be described as hybrids.

In Dramatic Painting we are brought face to face with the effect of some critical moment of time, when a tragic event has just happened or is about to happen when the world is illuminated with some sudden flash of light, or darkened by a shadow that will the next instant have altered or vanished.   In Dramatic Painting the expression must be forcible as the subject is instantaneous.

Yet this force must never degenerate into violence,

elaboration in a series of lectures, which it is to be hoped may soon become accessible in print.

or instead of the dramatic we shall produce the
theatrical. A contrast of light and shade is the most
potent vehicle for producing a dramatic effect; yet,
when the contrast is forced overmuch, the result will
be vulgar. Much of the once popular art of Gustave
Doré fails from the obvious artifice with which masses
of improbably bright light are opposed to masses
of improbably black shadow. The dramatic effect of
Spanish painting of the seventeenth century depends
upon a more realistic use of similar oppositions.
These forced effects are made still worse if they are
coupled with an attempt to suggest strong relief. The
paintings of such men as J. P. Laurens in modern
France, or in a less aggravated degree, much of the
work of Tintoret, and the later frescoes of Raphael (as
in the Chamber of the *Heliodorus*) are open to objection
on this score. The effect in these cases may be
powerful, but it lacks the repose that is an essential
condition of all supreme art.

As mentioned elsewhere, many, if not all, great
artists have, at an early period of their career, experi-
mented in dramatic effects, and in the course of their
experiments have sometimes been guilty of exaggeration. The dramatic darkness of Turner's *Calais Pier*
comes perilously near to theatricality; while the early
work of Rembrandt is full of examples in which the
artifice is even more conspicuous. The larger plate of
The Raising of Lazarus and the so-called *Hundred*

Guilder Plate might be quoted as cases in which force of contrast, skilful treatment of relief, with great powers of invention and draughtsmanship combine to produce results that are insincere precisely because they are so obviously effective. Titian's ceiling panels in the Salute show that his marvellous judgment was not invariably proof against the temptation, and even Velasquez in his early work is not always impeccable.

However, when rightly understood, the dramatic sense is of immense importance to the painter's equipment : indeed the man who lacks it altogether will always be a somewhat ineffective creature, whatever charm or skill he may possess. On a small scale, and where the subject calls for exceptional vigour, the strongest contrasts of tone may be safely used so long as they are not accompanied by attempts at relief,— that is to say, so long as the masses are comparatively flat. The aquatints of Goya and the lithographs of Daumier are admirable instances of this kind of emphatic statement. In painting, the oppositions must be more moderate, and the condition of low relief must be even more rigorously observed, as the mature paintings of Titian, Rembrandt and Velasquez will indicate.

Strong oppositions of colour, too, will help in producing a dramatic effect, even without the backing of oppositions of tone. In the pictures of Rubens, and in such works by Titian as the *Entombment* in the Louvre, the dramatic effect of contrasted tones is enhanced by that of contrasted colours, while some additional force is discreetly given by strong modelling. Delacroix always and Reynolds frequently use colour as an intensifying agent, combined with strong chiaroscuro, the latter element in the case of Reynolds being admirably illustrated by the mezzotints made from his portraits. In Constable's sketches, as the engravings by Lucas prove, a dramatic scheme of chiaroscuro underlies a colouring which is frequently the reverse of dramatic. In the prints of Hokusai dramatic effect is more scientifically and perfectly attained by means of colour contrasts aided by grand and audacious design; while in a portrait by Rembrandt we see the exact contrary. Here the colour is often hardly more than a pleasant monochrome, and the dramatic effect depends almost wholly upon light and shade.

Dramatic painting, being essentially the art of a swiftly passing crisis, is often concerned with active motion, yet in its noblest forms it treats that crisis, that activity, with a certain restraint. It is in plays appealing to the mob that the tragic climax of the plot is presented on the stage with its natural accompaniments of violence and blood. In the higher types of drama (though there are notable exceptions), the tendency is to avoid the actual perpetration of brutalities. The horror of the moment before the blow is struck, or of the moment after, is sufficient for the needs of art —on the moment itself the curtain may rightly fall.

Something of this reticence is commonly found in true dramatic painting. The great masters know that a crisis is most memorably suggested by the suspense of the moment inevitably leading to the fatal blow, or by the pity of the instant after the blow is given: they leave it to the sensationalist and the incompetent to strip the event of all its fascination by emphasising only the ugly prosy fact. A storm while advancing is impressive with the suggestion of terrible things to come; while retiring it may suggest terrible things that have just happened. When it is actually bursting upon us it conveys nothing but personal discomfort. The subject-matter of dramatic painting is effective or the reverse in precisely the same way.

Although we cannot assign any definite date as marking the actual birth of any of these forms of artistic feeling—they are implied in the beginning of art itself—we shall not be far from the truth if we assume that, so far as Europe is concerned, Lyrical Painting, as an independent product, really came into being in fifteenth-century Florence with such temperaments as Piero di Cosimo, and acquired definite position with Giorgione and Correggio. Of these two masters Giorgione has been the more influential, partly because his was the more abrupt rupture with preceding tradition, and partly because his immediate heir and successor was Titian. The lyrical element in

Titian's art refines the work of Velasquez and Van Dyck, and from Van Dyck descends to Gainsborough In landscape it inspires Claude, softens the rigidity of Poussin, and descends from them to Turner and Corot.

Watteau seems to create independently, for the lyrical element in his teacher Rubens is usually overwhelmed by other ideals. In Prudhon, however, we find a direct descendant of Correggio, and from Prudhon come Millet and Fantin. With the Dutch landscape painters, always excepting Rembrandt, it appears as a development or a consequence of an art which is for the most part essentially narrative, Matthew Maris in our own day being one of the rare exceptions. In the classical painting of China and Japan the lyrical mood is the predominant one, and intrudes itself frequently even when the subject is ostensibly anything but lyrical.

The list of names associated with Lyrical Painting will convey an idea of its character. It is before all things contemplative. It does not attempt to stir our feelings by the conflict of opposing forces, or to impress them with ideas of divine or human grandeur, but to charm us into sympathy with the artist's mood as he ponders upon the strangeness of things—their suggestiveness, their delightfulness, or their melancholy. In Dramatic Painting we are presented with a moment of swift and significant change. In Lyrical Painting the crisis is more remote ; time moves more slowly ; the world has leisure for happiness, and if there be clouds they cannot burst until we have had our fill of contemplating their menace.   In excess this contemplation becomes sentimentality, as the dramatic turns to melodrama.   Yet even a slight of hint of lyrical feeling will redeem work which would otherwise be prosy : while in its perfection it is responsible for the most charming works of art in the world, if not for the most grand or powerful.

To analyse in detail the immense variety and scope of its manifestations, or the accompanying technical conditions, is impossible in this place.   It will be enough to say that where Dramatic Painting relies upon contrast of masses and contours, of light and shade and colour, Lyrical Painting relies upon harmony. In the one we have force and abruptness ; in the other subtlety and gradation.   In the one the forms and the colours tend to be determinate ; in the other they are blended and combined.   This difference is continually forgotten or ignored with disastrous results : as in the countless pastoral landscapes where hard green grass and trees, hard white sheep or cattle, hard red roofs and hard blue sky, clash with each other, and destroy all ideas of harmony and quiet.

In the chapter dealing with the evolution of the artist, it is pointed out how the common practice of painters has been to begin with definition and contrast,

and to end with harmony and fusion. The fact seems
to indicate that the lyrical mood demands more skill
and experience from the artist than does the dramatic
—indeed, the sensitiveness of touch needed for subtle
gradation of colour, and the knowledge needed for the
securing of perfect fusion, are among the rarest of
artistic gifts ; far more rare than the power of conceiv-
ing and suggesting a dramatic effect. It is for this
reason, perhaps, that the most exquisite masters of
technique are to be found among the lyrical painters.
We cannot convey subtle or delicate feeling in art
without a corresponding quality in our workmanship:
hence the unsatisfactory results of our modern rough
and ready technical methods, and the difficulty of attaining lyrical expression through them.

With Satiric Painting we may deal no less briefly for
two reasons. In the first place, it has rarely been
supported by influential patronage, and with few exceptions has not been practised by the greatest painters.
Satire is essentially the protest of the weak against the
strong—of the subject against his masters. It is most
effective, too, when it serves the need of a particular
moment, and has for its object a particular person,
class or system. When that temporary purpose is
once accomplished, its mission is practically over: the
satire loses the freshness of its first significance and
becomes a historical curiosity.

Yet in a few of its manifestations Satiric art develops excellences which are not always found in painting with a much higher ostensible name; as in the case of Peter Bruegel the elder, by whom satire is enveloped with a mantle of impressiveness and majesty not unworthy of the greatest subjects. Jan Steen, too, as Reynolds has noted, often shows something of the same dignity. Satire, however, from its character and origin, rarely finds expression by means so elaborate as oil painting. Hogarth, Goya and Daumier, it is true, painted satiric pictures, but they all found a more effective and appropriate medium for their ridicule in engraving. With the etching and aquatint of Goya, and the lithography of Daumier, we may group the more genial caricature of Gillray and Rowlandson, and the slighter humours of nineteenth-century pen and ink work. Japan too has a long succession of witty draughtsmen in black and white, of whom Hokusai is the most generally known outside his own country.

All these different achievements in Satiric art are animated by a common spirit of lively emphasis—an emphasis obtained usually, if not quite invariably, by swift exuberant line work rather than by tone or colour. In the fiercer mood of a Daumier or a Goya this line work may be strengthened by forcible contrasts of light and shadow. Colour, too, is used lightly and playfully by Rowlandson as an ornament rather than as a reinforcement of his purpose. Still the essence of all

Satiric art seems to be the spontaneous vigorous use of line. Every detail or enrichment, not absolutely necessary to the production of that vigour and spontaneity detracts something from the force of the satire, as we see in the case of Hogarth's paintings, where we forget his moral intentions in admiration of his artistic charm. His engravings hit harder, because there his ridicule is seen in isolation, unadorned with attractive colour or felicitous brushwork.

As the satirist may bring unbounded exaggeration to his aid, he is of all artists the one who can most justly give free rein to his imagination, and may indulge in a corresponding freedom in the matter of design. He alone has the right of being absurd and extravagant, while the very simplicity and directness necessary for the delivery of an effective blow preserve him from most of the technical perils that beset more elaborate aims. His one practical difficulty is that of applying the thickest possible coat of pictorial tar and feathers, and yet leaving the victim recognisable under it. As a general rule those who have a real sense of humour and the slightest power of drawing, possess with them instinctive pictorial taste and good sense in expressing their wit, which does much to make amends for their inexperience.

Under the head of Narrative Painting we may include all those forms of art which aim at the representation of natural facts or appearances without laying stress on any particular characteristic, or group of characteristics, as the other forms of painting do. The Dramatic painter, the Lyrical painter, and the Satirist all select from nature certain qualities which it is their aim to isolate and emphasise. The Narrative painter, on the other hand, aims at describing in paint the sum total of the things nature presents to his sight, without omitting or accentuating any of them more than the rest.

Of all forms of painting it is the one of which the excellence can be most easily tested by comparison with the thing described. Probably for this reason it is the form of painting in which the uneducated public has taken most pleasure, and which it still regards as the crown and culmination of the painter's genius. Any veritable *trompe l'œil*, anything represented so clearly that it looks as if it could be touched or taken up, has for such persons the appearance of a miracle, and this ideal of deceptive resemblance persists even in quarters which we might expect to be better informed.

During the last century there have been moments when both painters and critics themselves seemed to share this view, as in the days of Ruskin and the Pre-raphaelites, though an overwhelming consensus of educated opinion has steadily condemned it, and the example of all the great masters is consistently opposed to it.

When viewed in historical perspective these apparent

exceptions explain themselves. Realistic movements are then seen to be no more than rebellions or reactions from the abuse or exhaustion of more liberal theories. It was in this spirit that Constable protested against the futile imitations of Claude and Poussin which passed current at the beginning of the nineteenth century, and the Pre-raphaelites broke away from the effete and petty historical painters half a century later. We notice, too, that the finest works produced under the influence of this reactionary enthusiasm are those which most perfectly subordinate the principle of literal imitation to the larger principles of rhythm and emphasis which underlie all pictorial excellence. Brett's *Val d'Aosta*, where everything is sacrificed to literal imitation, is a more marvellous, complete and truthful rendering of nature than Millais's *Sir Isumbras at the Ford*, which is from first to last a brilliant compromise between nature and pictorial effect. Yet Brett's picture now is seen to be only a most curious, accomplished and interesting *tour de force*, while Millais' *Sir Isumbras*, compromise though it be, is an immortal painting.

Indeed the great artists of all periods, though they have had the highest regard for truth, have never regarded truth as identical with deceptive imitation: though this fallacious identity, as we have seen, has generally been accepted by the public, and has provided it with an obvious and plausible critical formula. Leonardo's notes on painting show that the eyes of

quattrocento Florence could see the effect of bright
sunlight upon colour precisely as the Impressionists
saw it some four hundred years later. Yet in painting,
Leonardo used only such a fractional part of this knowledge and observation as was necessary and appropriate
for his pictures ; and when we come to the recognised
masters of realism the same principle is observed,
although the deliberate omissions are fewer than with
the Florentines.

In Northern Europe the minute handling proper to
the Flemish method of oil painting, coupled no doub'
with a somewhat matter-of-fact habit of mind, led first
to a precise and conscientious rendering of detail, and
afterwards in Holland to a display of imitative dexterity,
by which, with the lesser talents, the sense of pictorial
design is overwhelmed. Yet no such accusation can
be brought against the great masters of Narrative
Painting, such as John Van Eyck among the Flemings,
Holbein among the Germans (Dürer's brooding imagination places him for all his wealth of natural detail
rather among lyrical artists), Chardin among the French,
Terborch De Hoogh, Vermeer and Metsu among the
Dutch. If their general aim from first to last is a precise
and searching statement of natural facts, that statement
in all their best work is still kept rigorously subordinate
to the effect of the painting as a whole ; and, when they
meet with some aspect of nature which would conflict
with that effect, they alter or omit it without hesitation.

No man, perhaps, has seen the outward aspect of the human face more distinctly than Holbein and delineated it more unflinchingly. Our best modern portraiture would look clumsy or weak by the side of his, at once so minute and so grandly comprehensive; so alive to each variation of surface and contour; so resolute in including all those variations in one large subtle sweep of line or tender shadow. Yet in a good modern portrait we see much that we never see in a portrait by Holbein, namely, the thousand and one changes of tone and hue, caused by the reflection of the light of the sky or from surrounding objects. As mere imitations of nature these modern portraits must be regarded as in some ways more accurate than Holbein's, but no intelligent person could consider them better pictures.

All considerable artists have recognized how rigorous are the limits within which exact realism can be safely or profitably employed. So long as imitation of nature is conducive to the outward visual charm of a picture —to the enhancing of its decorative quality—so long and no longer is it valuable and admissible. The moment it conflicts with that decorative quality it becomes a source of danger. If it emerges from the conflict a victor, or even upon equal terms, the work has ceased to be a true picture and has become an illustration.

Even when conducted on sound lines, the province of Narrative Painting might seem but a small territory in comparison with the wide horizons that lie open before imaginative art. Yet in one respect at least it merits the attention even of imaginative artists. Their work, while retaining a pleasant decorative outward appearance, may become empty or conventional. To express their ideas they often need symbols of a somewhat abstract character, and those symbols may in course of time degenerate into mannerisms. The artist then will perhaps continue to secure pictorial unity, although the figures in his pictures have become mere artificial anatomies, and the landscape a mere drawing-master's flourish. It is then that Narrative Painting may come with its full-blooded, living and breathing humanity, its sunny, windy landscapes, to refresh and vitalize an exhausted conventional tradition. Its intrinsic capacities may be limited, but its indirect influence upon other forms of art has perhaps been even more important than the best things which it has itself achieved.

It sets up continually a standard of fulness of content without which no tradition, however great its primal vigour, can live long. When we speak of the decline of any school of painting, we are wont to do so in terms which imply a real mental degeneration in its later members, and we may be right. But a degeneration is so invariably accompanied by the loss of fulness of content, that we may be tempted to speculate whether the disease itself might not be cured or palliated, if this characteristic symptom could be removed by a little common sense.

For we cannot attribute the failure of great traditions wholly to mental inferiority in the painters who inherited them. If we think of the names once famous which now are found only in works of reference, or resound emptily in the older treatises of the arts (as do those of Placido Costanza, Pompeo Batoni, Imperiale and Sebastian Conca in the "Discourses" of Reynolds), we must remember that they were often men of considerable skill and talent. They inherited the pictorial formulæ of their greater predecessors, and they were not intellectually incapable of using them, but the results they achieved are insufferably tedious to posterity, just because those formulæ were never refreshed by the application of living nature which narrative art supplies. The classical art of China and Japan sometimes tends to be empty in a similar manner and for similar reasons. At present our painters do not suffer from this particular danger. The majority have erred rather in the opposite direction, and Narrative Painting, though it is a splendid tonic, is proving an intolerable diet. How the artist may most safely free himself from its ill effects must be discussed in a future chapter.

In this classification we have followed the painter from his genesis in the savage state, through his deriod of subjection to kings and priests, to the ages of individual freedom. It would be rash, or at least premature, to follow him further, to the stage when the painter becomes a member of that universal social fellowship with which, according to some authorities, we may shortly expect to be blessed.

Then pictures painted for the People will supersede pictures painted either for the painter's own pleasure or for that of any private patron ; such pictures, indeed, already exist in some quantity.   Yet if their existence entitles Socialist Painting to a place in our survey beside the examples of Despotic and Individual Painting which we possess, their present quality is not a very happy augury for the future of art under a collectivist régime. It will be enough to say that the one class of painting which may truly be described as painted for the People, chosen by the People's representatives, and paid for by the People, is that which forms the backbone of all our Colonial and Municipal Galleries, with three exceptions, but which is perhaps most favourably represented by the Chantrey Bequest purchases at Millbank.

The great painter, in fact, cannot be a Socialist. He must be at once an individualist and a servant. An individualist, because it is unlikely that a tradition will arise in these days in which he can profitably allow his personal talent and character to be submerged. Only a tradition comparable to that of Greek Sculpture would justify such a sacrifice, and such traditions are born of needs more magnanimous and more consistent than any which the modern painter of easel pictures is called upon to supply. He must be a servant too, in that he must fulfil certain decorative conditions, settled neither by himself, nor usually by his rulers or patrons, but by the habits and customs of his age. Mural paintings are so rarely commissioned that not one painter in a thousand can produce anything but easel pictures, or do otherwise than adapt his largest ideals to their modest scale and to the functions easel pictures are wont to perform.

But this very service, this process of adaptation, taking a new shape with each different mind and every fresh requirement, propounds an infinity of problems to engage the painter's wits, and to stimulate him to novel inventions, to combinations never before achieved. Nor can this service be regarded as other than honourable, as a part, indeed, of the artist's bounden duty, if we remember how even Michelangelo bowed to such compulsion in its most harsh and oppressive form, and was ordered away from the sculpture which he loved to paint the Sistine Ceiling.

CHAPTER XVIII

THE PAINTER'S TRAINING

I HAVE insisted more than once on the comparative failure of art criticism; the failure of art education has, perhaps, been even more conspicuous. In proportion to the money lavished by Governments and the energy lavished by experts upon training artists, the results are deplorably small. Thousands upon thousands of enthusiasts, not lacking ability, have been prepared for the painter's calling; yet not one in fifty, on a generous computation, has left any memorial that was worth leaving. On the contrary, a large part of the art products which we now value are the work of men whose education was, to the outward eye, imperfect; and who succeeded not because they followed their teachers, but because they defied them.

If, when surveying the development of artists during the last five hundred years, we could discover no common tendency, no regular process of growth, we might indeed despair—we might assume that the talent of the painter is something apart from all ordinary intellectual laws; that it can neither be fostered by

methodical encouragement, nor be crushed by un-
sympathetic surroundings; and that in consequence
the gigantic wastage and extravagance which have
accompanied all systems of art-teaching are inevitable.
But in one respect at least this is not the case.

That there is a certain sequence in the stages of the
artist's evolution has long been a matter of common
knowledge, though, so far as I am aware, it has not
been very carefully analysed. Nearly all great artists
have begun by working with some precision. This
precision gradually towards middle life is modified by
a desire for greater breadth of mass; this desire, in its
turn, is exchanged on the approach of old age for a
love of freedom of brush work, and a disregard for all
minor details. So universal is this development that,
in ninety-nine cases out of a hundred, it enables a
painting by a great artist to be referred at once to the
period of his work in which it was produced, without
the need of adducing external evidence.

In basing our current ideas of art training upon this
generally recognized course of individual development,
we do rightly; for we have no other ground at all
upon which a working system could be logically
founded. Yet the results for the last three hundred
years have been so poor that we may well ask whether
there is not a misunderstanding somewhere at the
root of things which has vitiated our whole educational
tradition.

Our eyes are so powerfully attracted by the supreme masters of the Renaissance, that we naturally think that the system which produced a Michelangelo, a Titian, and a Raphael, must also be the one best adapted to our students of to-day. But are we quite able to reconcile the universal application of this system with the growth of a Rembrandt, a Goya, a Daumier, or a Rossetti? Are we not bound to recognize that, if there be one great group of artists who must be regarded as the direct heirs or exponents of a classical tradition, there is also another, including at least an equal number of famous names, of artists who in comparison are romantics, reactionaries or rebels. Moreover, during the last hundred years this second group has been infinitely more powerful and important than the first. All our systems of teaching the arts have been derived from the practice of the former group; no one seems to have attempted to elucidate the general principles underlying the activities of the latter.

The essential difference between the two groups lies in their contrasted attitudes towards tradition. Raphael and Titian were born into a world where a definite technical practice of using tempera, oil and fresco had been gradually built up, though no painter had as yet succeeded in solving by its help certain difficult problems of representation. Thus quite apart from any imaginative aims, these great masters of the full Renaissance had to gird themselves to the task of carrying to completion that mastery of natural appearances which their predecessors had failed to attain. That mastery once secured, all the pictorial resources of their time and country lay at their feet, to be transmuted into perfect art, once and for ever.

So we find Raphael in boyhood acquiring all the skill of his master Perugino. Then, at Florence, he applies himself to study the construction, motion and mass of the human body, till in the Borghese *Entombment* he appears to his contemporaries to have excelled the Florentines in their own special province. Even when summoned to Rome, the first of his frescoes, the *Disputà*, is still Umbro-Florentine. Increased knowledge of classical antiquity gives weight to *The School of Athens;* in the *Parnassus* it is made serene and joyous decoration; to the *Mass of Bolsena* Venetian influence brings new contact with humanity and a new glow of colour. Then, just when the painter seemed to have learned all that was necessary to the perfection of his genius, the goddess of Discord threw down her fatal fruit.

Forced by Roman party spirit into competition with Michelangelo's Sistine Ceiling in the chapel hard by, and harried incessantly by the importunate admiration of his friends at the Papal Court, Raphael was deprived at once of the singleness of aim with which he had hitherto pursued his art, of the leisure required to think out the drastic changes in his ideas which rivalry with Michelangelo seemed to demand, and even of the time to paint his pictures with his own hand. No wonder then that the *Heliodorus* and its successors, designed without due reflection, and executed by heavy handed assistants from mere sketches, degrade the fame of Raphael. Had he lived the common span of human life—had fate ever allowed him a breathing space in which to contemplate the course of his own art—his equable reasonable genius was great enough to have turned upon itself, and to have recognized that this newly discovered chiaroscuro, which had been invoked to give additional force and movement, was a poison as well as a stimulant. So Raphael might have discovered at last, as Titian did in extreme old age, that chiaroscuro was a valuable servant only when ruled by a despot. Fate decided otherwise and, with the *Parnassus* and the *Mass of Bolsena*, Raphael's career as a painter ends.

Titian in the same way first masters the glowing science of the Bellinesque practice, and then immensely enlarges both his mental and technical experience by contact with Giorgione. Much of the older Venetian sense of vivid colour pattern survives even in works like the *Bacchus and Ariadne*, where his powers are seen at perhaps their most delightful moment. Then, like Raphael, he is attracted towards chiaroscuro, as a means of getting still further force and solidity of modelling, and for many years suffers from similar difficulties ; acquiring only in extreme old age the secret of that subtle fusion of broken tones, of which the great *Pietà* in the Venice Academy is the most famous and familiar example.

We might summarise the lessons drawn from the history of these two great masters somewhat as follows :

(1) They begin by almost slavish assimilation of the precise yet imperfect style of their masters.

(2) Round this nucleus they gradually accumulate other experiences, Raphael advancing by far the more rapidly, till, with the view of mastering the final problems of complete representation, they attempt to combine strong chiaroscuro with colour. While still struggling with this difficulty Raphael dies.

(3) Titian continues the struggle, and in extreme old age finds that the solution lies not in forcible contrasts of dark and light, or of vivid colours, but in the subtle fusion of broken and indefinite tones.

If we compare this progress with the development of Turner, we shall find exactly the same order of advance. First, we have the imitations of Cozens and Girtin, of Claude and Poussin and Backhuysen; with such experiments in chiaroscuro as the *Calais Pier* and *Liber Studiorum*. The difficulties of combining this chiaroscuro with colour are seen in the plates of the "Harbours of England," as their conquest is seen in the "Rivers of France," which prepare the way for the supreme subtlety and fusion of Turner's old age.

These masters, it must be noted, were all born into the world at a time when the particular tradition from which they started was imperfect. The Florentine tradition was just short of full ripeness when Raphael came to Florence; the Bellinesque tradition was still splendidly young when Titian was born in Venice; landscape was still to all intents and purposes a toy or an appanage of figure painting when Turner and Constable arose to reveal its independent power. When with the full Renaissance the power of complete representation of the human form had been acquired, a new Raphael or a new Titian was impossible. When Turner and Constable had done with landscape they left little or nothing for their successors to do on the same lines. Each field of artistic activity, in fact, is exhausted by the first great artist who gathers a full harvest from it.

The task of those born after great periods of discovery and achievement is thus entirely different, and perhaps more difficult, than that of men born in earlier ages, when the whole world lay open to the ambitious mind. A few immensely gifted celebrities like Van Dyck and Reynolds have been saved, in spite of themselves, by the necessity which drove them to restrict their talents to the ever-fresh, if narrow, province of portraiture; but with more imaginative intellects this restriction was not possible.

Of these intellects, Rembrandt is the first and the

greatest. He comes into the world to find the science of representative painting, in the form understood by the men of his time, already so complete that except in details no further advance seemed practicable. The science of religious and historical painting was equally complete to the outward eye; but there the native feeling of the Dutch race for honest portrayal of real persons and things had been overwhelmed by Italian influence, and the current generalisations of design and contour possessed neither the spirit of a living art, nor the elegance which in Southern Europe disguised this age of emptiness and decay.

Unable to develop with profit either the realist or the imaginative tradition of his time, Rembrandt had no option but to revolt from them. So soon as his portraits become complete examples of all-round realism (and that costs him no small effort), he must move a step further ; and he does so by emphasizing a particular characteristic of his sitters—the inevitable isolation of the human soul. To suggest this detachment from all the things and thoughts of this earth, he sacrifices the pleasant light of the sun, he sacrifices colour and all the common apparatus of pictorial charm, with the result that he secures a mastery of certain aspects of human personality which remains supreme and unique. Like all forms of emphatic statement it was misunderstood and despised by his contemporaries ; his practice

S

as a portrait painter in consequence languished, and he died a forgotten pauper.*

Rembrandt's attitude towards the imaginative art of his time was no less decided. That art was lifeless; he determined that his own work should at all costs be full of life. Instead of the graceful Raphaelesque ideals of the time, he introduced real persons, the members of his own family and household, and the beggars from the street. The difficulty of obtaining any models at all in Holland probably contributed to his determination to draw largely upon his memory, and the gradual training of that marvellous memory is not the least profitable lesson to be learnt from his etched work.† The result of this defiance of generalised beauty, this trust in life and nature, is that Rembrandt's subject-pieces are as solitary and supreme in their sympathy with human character as are his portraits.

In the matter of design, Rembrandt's revolt was no less emphatic. To escape from the suave but insipid patterns of the Italianizers, he went to the opposite extreme of abruptness and contrast; hence the melodramatic oppositions of light and darkness which are characteristic of his early style. With growing experience this obvious and forcible rhythmic contrast

* For a fuller account of Rembrandt's attitude towards portraiture, see the *Burlington Magazine*, Jan. 1908, vol. xii. pp. 197–8.

† See the *Burlington Magazine*, May, July, August, and October 1906, vol. ix. pp. 87, 245, 313 38

gives place (as with Titian and Turner), to the subtle fusion which distinguishes all his later products.

Now, when we survey the career of other great reactionaries—Tiepolo, Goya, Daumier, Delacroix, Blake, Rossetti, Millet, Puvis de Chavannes—men working like Rembrandt, in the midst of tired conventionalism or tired realism, we find in all of them this same adoption of a more vigorous and simple rhythm, a more definite emphasis of certain parts of nature, instead of any attempt at an all-round compromise. Did space allow, it would be easy to prove the case in detail; but those who have followed me thus far will recognise its truth without further explanation.

In effect, then, the development of the individual artist would seem to take a course corresponding to that of the human race.

(1) It must have, first of all, its primitive stage. Where art is already in an immature state, this stage is that in which the artist finds himself at birth and from which he develops naturally, as the great artists of the early Renaissance developed.

Where art is already ripe, where the science of representation is perfectly understood, a réturn must be made to the primitive state, or the painter's after-growth will be warped. To continue the tradition of a mature period is like being born middle-aged. Primitive art, as we have seen, is characterised by a strong sense of vitality, and still more by emphatic rhythm of pattern.

(2) This primitive vigour may afterwards find vent in Dramatic Painting (as boys write heavy tragedies), and may be constantly varied by experiments towards increasing the realistic element, experiments similar to those made by Raphael, Titian and Rembrandt when they attempted to combine strong modelling with strong local colour.

(3) Finally, towards the end of an artist's career, these experiments terminate in a desire for fusion—for the creation of a pictorial atmosphere in which all the various elements of the design are harmoniously enveloped. Art, in fact, ceases to be dramatic, and becomes lyrical. Often, however, by the time this stage is reached, failing health involves some loss of power. Only in rare cases is a painter's late work so uniformly valuable as that of his early and middle life. So an old civilisation learns the art of refined living, but loses at the same time its creative and military effectiveness.

Such practical conclusions as may be deduced from this study of the career of our predecessors do not amount to much more than is already recognised by all intelligent art teachers, except in one or two respects, and may be summed up as follows :

The common practice of teaching an artist to draw and paint precisely and accurately at the outset of his career is absolutely correct. All great artists have started by mastering the science of representation. No one at all has, I believe, succeeded by beginning where the great masters leave off, that is to say, by aiming at fusion before learning definition.

Where the practice of the past differs from that of the present is in the use of models. The custom of to-day is to teach the painter to rely upon models entirely, both for the figure and for landscape. The old masters, on the other hand, consistently practised working from memory side by side with working from the model. They were thus able not only to keep their wits alert to counteract the mechanical habit of mind which grows upon those who work solely from models, but also were able to give solidity to the things which they imagined.

Next as to tradition. *The artist must never be content with the current tradition of his time.* To do so is to remain stationary ; and the artist must go forward at any cost If he is bred in an incomplete tradition, he will naturally attempt to carry it forward one stage nearer to completion. If the tradition of his time be already complete it has no further use for him. He must go back to the primitive elements of his art, rhythm and vitality, and use them as a base for an advance upon new and personal lines. The training of this new vigour, and the control of this new vitality will be his first business when his pupilage is over ; and, as years and experience increase, he will enrich his paintings with the fruits of his knowledge till they become complete and original works of art.

All great artists, however precocious their beginning, have been a long time in attaining to the summary breadth, fusion and emphasis of their final manner. This has seldom been adopted much before the artist's fiftieth year, even when the effort to evolve it has been incessant. Indeed the middle period of a painter's career would really seem to be the crucial one, and not, as is commonly supposed, the early period. There are plenty of instances of young painters whose school record was one of incompetence, but who in after years became great artists—the case of Constable is a striking example—while how many hundred painters who were once the pride of an art school, and seemed to have fame and fortune safely grasped, have disappeared from memory before they were forty!

The artist must remain a student all the time he is attempting to be a master. Breadth and freedom are not only passwords to praise from many critics, but to the unthinking they seem easier than laborious exactness, and the path from ease to indolence is short. The broad treatment which at first retained something of the sound knowledge amassed as a student, soon becomes a trick of hand, with nothing behind it. The mind is saved the trouble of thinking and at last loses the power of doing so from sheer want of exercise. For a time this leisurely shallowness may escape notice, and may even achieve some little success, but a day will come when comparison has to be made with more serious and thoughtful work, and the deception is found out.

And the case is hopeless. No instance I believe is known of a painter regaining the powers of his youth after he has once succumbed to the temptations of indolence or popularity. In other walks of life it is not uncommon to hear of men pulling themselves together in middle age, and regaining intellectual powers which had seemingly lapsed for want of exercise. But the peculiar blend of mental activity and manual skill which the art of painting demands is not so long-suffering. Not only does it never forgive the man who has once for any reason neglected it, but even those who try hardest to retain and develop their powers do not always succeed.

The best remedy for this prevalent perilous disease of middle age would seem to be endless exercise of the brain—endless experiment. That at least has been the practice of the great masters, whose work in middle life is a record of incessant change, incessant trial of new subjects and new methods, incessant alternation between working from the model and working from memory, until the period of experiment is succeeded by that of experience—of perfect knowledge.

How different is our contemporary art. There almost

every painter, so soon as his manner is known at all, is associated in the public mind with a particular class of subject and a particular treatment, from which any radical departure is received almost as a sacrilege. We have perhaps learned to regard youth as the period of exact scholarship, but, until we also regard middle age as the period of untiring experiment, we must not expect an artist after he is fifty to be anything but an object for pity and silence.

How far an artist is benefited by the society of his fellows or that of the world at large is a question answered by no universal precedent. If Michelangelo, Rembrandt, and Turner illustrate the coincidence of insight with isolation, the happier lives of Titian, and Rubens, and Reynolds might be quoted with equal justice to prove that high excellence is not incompatible with a wide acquaintance. All the same, the personal popularity of Raphael and Van Dyck injured their painting as it shortened their lives.

As a rule a man's personality, or his style of work, do more to decide his habits of life than any deliberate choice. An ungainly presence and uncouth manners will isolate their possessor; the profession of a portrait painter will forbid entire seclusion. The evidence of the past on the whole points to some measure of seclusion as necessary for those who wish to do great things, although if that seclusion become solitude both the painter and his work may suffer. Yet for one painter who has narrowed his art from lack of converse with his fellows, a hundred have ruined their work by going to the opposite extreme and taking social patronage too seriously.

The painter would do well in boyhood to frequent the company of his fellow students; from it he will derive some standard of skill, and perhaps some stimulus in discussion. In his later years he may mix with the world as much as he inclines; and he can then do so without the least danger, for his character will be formed and fixed. Only in early manhood and middle life will he imperatively need some times of solitude in which to think out the problems of his profession; and it is just then that the pleasures of the world are wont to be most importunate and most acceptable.

CHAPTER XIX

THE FUTURE OF PAINTING

ARTISTS themselves, and their critics too, are wont to act and speak as if the style and ideals of their own time were the last word in art—to regard themselves as enshrining a perfect tradition, from which any marked departure must be rank heresy. Few have been able to receive with enthusiasm the appearance of a style essentially different from their own. The whole record of painting during the last hundred years, has been a record of revolt and persecution—revolt by youthful talent against the degeneracy of some old tradition, answered by hostility and repression on the part of the seniors.

When the progress of the arts during the past century has been thus irregular, it would be unreasonable to expect it to be otherwise in the immediate future. Change seems to be a condition of all great achievement in the arts, for, as we have seen, it is usually by the pioneers of change that the greatest pictures are painted. No follower of Constable has attained anything like the same position : Delacroix,

Rousseau, Corot, Millet, have had no successors of equal force; the work done by Millais, Rossetti and their associates in their years of unpopularity has never been equalled; the best Impressionist pictures were painted long ago when their painter's names were a byword. A revolt then against an established style, instead of being received with the derision which is generally its fate, should be welcomed as the one possible source from which the arts may derive new vitality.

Not that mere novelty must of necessity be admirable The reproach of slightness brought against the work of the Impressionists was in a measure just. Constable's critics were not wholly wrong when they blamed the unpleasant substance and surface of some of his paintings; nor were those who found Pre-raphaelite colouring garish without some ground for their dislike. Yet these peculiarities were sacrifices necessary to the excellences of the works in question. It is only when the result does not justify the sacrifice, that we have any right to find serious fault. New excellence, new character, new emphasis, can rarely be attained without renouncing some quality which a previous generation has prized. The value of a new movement must be judged in relation to the importance of the message it brings, quite apart from the sacrifices which the artist has had to make in order to deliver his message at all.

But painting is subject to changes of another kind

over which artists have no control. These changes may be described as changes of patronage and of function. Of patronage in so far as the artist is usually dependent upon selling his pictures to some one else: of function in that pictures serve a decorative purpose, and have a definite relation to architecture. In one age the artist will be employed in covering the walls of palaces, in another he will be compelled to devote his talent to producing small easel pictures for private houses.

So far as function is concerned we can speculate with some certainty as to the immediate future. Whatever political and social commotions may be in store for us, we may assume that the present diffusion of wealth, while it may shift its locality, will not be materially altered in character. The majority of picture buyers will continue to live in houses much like those of to-day, while the convenience of being able to move the ordinary framed easel picture from one house to another will probably cause this form of art to retain its present vogue.

Of recent years great improvements have been effected in the setting of prints and drawings, so that even slight sketches and studies can be transformed by tactful mounting and framing into real decorative units. It would seem to follow that these slighter forms of art would be viewed with ever-increasing favour. Their moderate prices will be an inducement to many who can never afford to collect important pictures, while the light and cheerful effect of framed drawings will often suit our sunny modern interiors better than the heavier tones of oil painting.

In the framing of oil pictures we have so far been much less successful.   Many pictures seem to look best in frames which are themselves neither beautiful nor harmonious with other furniture.   The pictures of the Barbizon school for instance, are almost invariably set in frames which have an undeniably vulgar look. Yet in such a rectangle of gilded contortion, a Corot or a Daubigny shows to perfection : place it in a frame of more reticent design, and it becomes in a moment flat, empty and tame.   This matter of framing must in the future receive far more serious attention than has been paid to it hitherto, for in no quarter is attention more needed, or more immediately bound up with practical success.

As to the future of patronage it is less easy to speak, the support of the Fine Arts being intimately dependent upon political and social conditions which cannot be forecast with certainty.   We may be tolerably sure that future wars, however exhausting internecine and disastrous to individual states, will not result in such an overthrow of the organisation, comfort and intellectual activity of civilised life, as took place when the Roman Empire of the West fell upon evil days. The arts have ceased to be the property of any single state; and the printing press has diffused the great mass of human knowledge so widely that no political or social upheaval can quite overwhelm it.

The number of people who profess a general liking for the fine arts has certainly increased with the spread of printed matter. Many more thousands may visit the Royal Academy than was the case half a century ago, just as many more thousands read and write, but it may be doubted whether the pictures which those thousands really admire can reach any higher standard than the magazines and halfpenny papers which form their literary diet. We must presume the continuity of education; we must presume also the continuity, if not the steady increase, of this large class of untrained admirers, and with it the continuity of means for gratifying their admiration.

In comparison with this vast assemblage of uncritical spectators, the number of those who possess sound taste, and the means of gratifying it by the purchase of works of art, will probably remain small. In England, at the present moment, it appears to be even smaller than the general wealth of the country would warrant, and the few who would like to collect pictures for their own sake are compelled to regard their purchases more or less in the light of an investment.

The most casual study of sale-room records brings the collector face to face with the striking fact that pictures by well-known Royal Academicians no longer fetch at Christie's a twentieth part of their original cost. Overlooking the fact that works of this particular class and this particular period were, at the time of their production, artificially inflated both in reputation and price, and that the opinion of all serious critics has been uniformly adverse to them, the collector argues from this collapse that no modern painting can be bought except with the probability of heavy loss, if circumstances ever compel its appearance in the market.

On the other hand he sees the finest works, whether old or modern, fetching higher and higher prices, which place them as much out of his reach on the ground of first cost, as the sale room records seem to place modern pictures out of it on the ground of ultimate depreciation. Our newly-developed outdoor pastimes too, are often expensive and successful rivals to intellectual pursuits, with which true picture-collecting must be classed.

In direct opposition to these forces retarding the purchase of all modern pictures (except portraits which have the impregnable support of human vanity), is the steady absorption of fine works of art, either into great public collections, or into private collections from which they are never likely to emerge. The available masterpieces are not inexhaustible, and the competition displayed during the past few years over the comparatively few good pictures which have been sold, indicates that the time is not far distant when the only works by deceased masters which even a rich collector can obtain will be works of the second rank.

For a time these inferior works will, no doubt, be forced upon the market, but publicity will make comparisons inevitable, and it will become evident that the best modern work is undeniably better than the second best work of the past. Good work by living men will then have to be collected because there is nothing else to collect. In the narrow field of etching this process has already begun, and plates by the best modern masters are in steady demand, and fetch good prices, because print collectors have discovered that the old masters are now quite beyond the reach of modest purses.

This forecast applies only to the very best work, and immediately only to such phases of it as have some note of continuity with accepted traditions. Whatever their intrinsic merit, the most original pictures, from their very originality, may still have to wait some time for recognition; as will those which, from their size or subject-matter, do not suit modern rooms or are remote from contemporary taste. Yet the lack of quite first rate pictures is already becoming so marked that, in a few years time, it may even overwhelm these minor obstacles, and make real talent practically sure of a modest competence.

More than that it would be unwise to hope for. Great prices are paid by great collectors only for works which have stood the test of time, and are stamped with the hall-mark of generally recognised excellence. Work which has not stood this test lies outside the great collectors' province, and does not enter that expensive domain until it has passed with credit through one or two minor collections. The price the artist himself receives will still be but a small fraction of that which will ultimately be paid for his picture, and he may thus remain comparatively poor, at the very time when his early pictures fetch thousands of pounds.

While circumstances thus seem to be, on the whole, not unfavourable for the really good artist, the prospects of the painter who fails to attain unique prominence in some branch of his craft, are perhaps worse than they have ever been. Unless he cultivates the arts of the society portrait painter, or takes to illustration, he has little chance of making a living by his brush. While dealers and collectors like to have the very finest things, they have no interest whatever in pictures which do not reach their exacting standard, so that for all pictures, except the very best of their respective classes, there is no market at all. The spread of education may have slightly increased the number of casual purchasers and of small collectors, but this increase is far more than counterbalanced

T

by the gigantic growth in the number of professional painters.

The elements of the art of representing things in paint, can be more or less soundly learned in thousands of art schools. The mastery of these elements is not beyond the power of young gentlemen and young ladies of average intelligence: their possession, in an age devoted to naturalism, is enough to constitute a painter. The result is the immense multiplication of works which are skilful and conscientious up to a certain point, but are fundamentally commonplace, and cannot provide their makers with a living.

In the course of time governments may recognise that it is useless extravagance to train all who desire it for a profession in which not one in a hundred can be expected to do any practical good either to his country or to himself. If teaching were generally restricted to drawing alone, and further training permitted only to those, whatever their age, who could produce some certificate of exceptional inventive or executive power, a large amount of energy now lost to the world might be diverted into more useful if more prosaic channels.

Already the more talented artists all the world over have recognised the danger, and are making spasmodic efforts to cope with it, realising that they serve their reputations ill by allowing their works to be buried in large shows where the majority of the pictures are bad. We may thus expect in the future a sharp division.

There will be comparatively small exhibitions of good pictures, with a small *clientèle* of collectors and persons of exceptional taste ; and there will be large exhibitions of inferior work, dependent upon the shillings of the uneducated public, where sales, except to municipal galleries and proprietors of popular journals, will be almost unknown.

It is no vain or unprofitable labour to discuss the material welfare and the æsthetic capacity of the artist's patrons. The one decides the limits of scale within which the painter has to express himself, and to some extent even the mediums he must use; the other at least influences him in matters of treatment, especially where departures from established custom are concerned. On the first point we have already seen that easel pictures of moderate size will have to be the medium of the artist's largest thoughts, except on rare occasions ; while drawing, etching, and the various forms of engraving will tend to increase in popularity. On the æsthetic capacity of future patronage depend more important and vital issues.

In a certain sense the artist is the teacher of his patrons. It is the artist who invents the new vision, the new executive formula and, until he has embodied his inventions in a picture, even the most intelligent of his contemporaries cannot begin to appreciate the value of the new qualities which he is introducing. Taste in the arts will never be quite an abstract intellectual faculty; it must always be founded upon and influenced by previously existing works of art. The painter who produces good pictures not only adds his canvases to the world's wealth, but in course of time adds to the world's culture the new knowledge and perception of which they are the embodiment.

As a rule, however, the acceptance of the new qualities which a good painter introduces is a slow process, even with the intelligent. Few really great and original artists during the last hundred years have been understood by, or have educated, even a small section of the public till they were past middle life. In youth they have almost invariably been subjected either to total neglect or to the charge of ugliness, the one word by which the uneducated can safely describe any departure from the pictorial symbols to which they are accustomed. But youth is a time when the mind is most plastic, and it is inevitable that all but the strongest must be influenced in early life by the views of the persons about them. Even if these persons be intelligent, a certain inertia has to be overcome before they can be brought to recognise an original departure in the arts, and the history of painting is full of memories of those who were not strong enough to conquer this opposition—men born out of due time, timid unsuccessful pioneers of movements that in a future generation, in the hands of more persistent and powerful champions, were to attain unquestioned triumph.

This inertia, this tardy acceptance of any departure from the current formulæ of painting, with the waste of talent which it involves, can never be wholly removed; but its powers of resistance might be much diminished, if its nature were more closely studied.

The great innovations which from time to time have refreshed the general tradition of the arts have all one common characteristic. Each has consisted, as we have seen, in the addition of new elements of vitality and rhythm to an art grown old and languid, and with these new elements there necessarily followed a new pictorial symbolism.

This vitality is, in a sense, cumulative, for each innovator's structure is made so much higher by starting from the ruins of his predecessor. Claude's landscape is more vital than that of Perugino, Turner than Claude; while the Pre-raphaelites and the Impressionists in their respective ways go farther than Turner. All the great movements in art, even when they appear most reactionary, even when their nostalgia—their passion for old forms of life or thought—is strongest, endow these past things with a vitality which they have never had before, so that their antique garb is but a cloak for the spirit and freshness of youth.

A new difficulty confronts us when we apply this principle to our speculation upon the course which pictorial invention will take in the future. We live in an age of unrestrained universal naturalism, when the representation of the phenomena of light and colour, as revealed in all visible things, has been made the subject of incessant study, and has perhaps been carried to as great a degree of completeness, in most directions, as is ever likely to be attained. How is it possible to add further vitality to an art of which Constable and Claude Monet were no more than the founders ? Must not every step in the future be a step backwards from the more or less complete representation of nature at which we have arrived ?

Were this so the prospects of the painter would indeed be melancholy, for he would have no more worlds to conquer. But, as indicated in the previous chapter, the expression of vitality is not confined to an all-round statement of things in themselves alive, but may be conveyed also, and often more effectively, by an emphatic statement of a few significant features. For example, many painters of peasant life have painted French fields, French skies, and French peasants with singular faithfulness and skill : yet not one of them has got so near to the heart of the toiling peasant as Millet did, by concentrating his attention upon just the significant facts and suppressing the rest. Whistler's superiority to other painters of London depends upon just the same concentrated emphasis of a few things, instead of an emphasis diluted by insistence on everything at once.

It is quite possible that the acceptance of this principle of concentrated emphasis and resolute sacrifice
may be accelerated by the introduction of some new
medium. There is no reason why the practice of the
future should be restricted to the commonly received
processes of representation in oil, tempera and water
colour. Efforts have already been made to revive
enamelling; can we not imagine that a similar effort
might succeed in reviving some such medium as
lacquer—limited perhaps in range of hue and in
manipulative ease, but compensating for these limitations by the perfection of its decorative quality?

Such a new medium might almost at once bring
about a widening of our æsthetic perceptions, though
the widening, unless it were based upon a foundation
of logic, might be no more permanent than it has
proved to be in Japan. Some great artist in stained
glass or mosaic might effect a similar revolution of
feeling.

In practice this process of unhesitating selection and
omission is open to one very real peril. It may be
carried so far that the residue left for pictorial expression is unduly small, and the picture, though decora-
tively perfect, will seem slight or empty when put by
the side of other paintings possessing more significant
subject-matter—more fulness of content. The later
works of Whistler are open to criticism on this ground.
All are exquisite and charming works of art which

convey their message perfectly, but the message itself is often next to nothing.

The classical painting of China and Japan errs in the same way, at least to Western eyes. Here we invariably find decorative effect, calligraphic dexterity, and often a large lyrical feeling, but to most of us its subject-matter will appear inadequate. Only when we come to the realistic masters, and especially to the Japanese colour-printers, do we begin to find enough subject-matter to justify a picture. We must, however, remember that the subject of a Chinese painting, which appears in our eyes so insignificant, is by no means insignificant in the eyes of the race for whom it was painted. Steeped in classical literature and poetry, the educated Oriental thinks, talks, and sees in terms of literary allusion. The rocks and water and clouds, the plants, the animals, and the personages which make the common subject-matter of Chinese art, have for a native audience a profound and complicated secondary significance which we cannot hope to understand. Their painters, in fact, have learned to paint for a race whose perceptions are so cultivated, that the merest suggestion of a natural object is enough to evoke in the mind a long train of pleasant associations.

In Europe it will be long before the artist can expect so much from his public. On the contrary the educated public at first, and the general public for many years will continue to treat the great artist as their predecessors treated his in the past. To them his emphasis of some particular vital quality in nature will appear as ugliness, and will be abused under that name; while the sacrifices he has made to obtain that emphasis will be condemned as incompleteness. Indeed so universally have terms "ugly" and "incomplete" been used in Europe to decry every phase of original art on its first appearance (now and then, as with the Pre-raphaelites, "incompleteness" has been replaced by "indecency"), that I believe it would be no bad rule for the collector who wishes to discover rising talent, to confine his study to those works by young men which were consistently damned by the critics of the baser sort as incomplete and ugly. If their technical merits were allowed he would be on still safer ground; while if their subject-matter also proved on examination to have some considerable charm or interest, he might feel secure that he was following real talent, and no mere will-o'-the-wisp.

The rock on which generation after generation of inconsiderate critics, and in particular all academies of the Fine Arts, have come to grief, is their habit of judging new works of art by some fixed standard of grace, or power, or proportion, established and determined by pictures already in existence. New pictures which correspond in some considerable degree to such a standard are therefore at once acclaimed as masterpieces; those that differ radically from this accepted

standard are called ugly. In reality this correspondence with some existing standard of grace, or power,
or proportion, is not a merit but a fatal defect. It
implies imitation, and no great artist ever was an
imitator after his student days. The great artist
invariably departs in some degree from the canons
and standards of his own age, and by that departure
creates a new quality which is at first suspected for
eccentricity, or attacked as ugliness ; but which in time
is understood, becomes in its turn a standard and is
everywhere recognised as beauty.

CHAPTER XX

SOME POPULAR FALLACIES

To avoid the risk of misapprehension, it may be well to recapitulate briefly the conclusions suggested by these notes on some points where the popular notions of painting seem to be unsettled.

For example, there is a constant hesitation in the popular mind as to whether the subject-matter of a picture, its inward significance, is more important than its technical expression, its outward decorative aspect. There can be no real doubt as to the truth. As music conveys its meaning to us through the ear, so a picture must convey its meaning to us through the eye. It is through the visible attractiveness of its pattern of inter-woven lines, and tones, and colours that we must be introduced to the significance of the images which that pattern includes. Decoration therefore has always a definite precedence over Significance in all good pictures. The moment the position is reversed; when a canvas appeals to the mind rather than to the eye; when we think of the story which it tells before our eyes have been gladdened by the attractiveness of its general appearance—when Significance, in short, has taken precedence of Decoration—the thing is an Illustration, not a Picture.

In many of the noblest achievements of art, as in the frescoes of Raphael, Significance and Decoration are so evenly balanced that the result is supreme illustration as well as supreme painting. The distinction between the two is more easily grasped when we deprive each in turn of its subordinate element.

In the case of a Picture, if we reduce Significance to a minimum we get ultimately to something like an Oriental Carpet; if, in the same way, we deprive Illustration of all decorative quality we get ultimately to a figure in Euclid.

The efforts of the best critics in all ages have been devoted, with but indifferent success, to impressing this radical distinction upon the public mind. Training is needed to appreciate the subtleties of design, form and colour, which are the elements of fine decoration ; just as training is needed to understand the subtleties of good music. But the general public will not take the trouble to learn the elements either of music or paint-ing ; it is content with the painting that tells an obvious story as it is with the music-hall song. The illus-trator, in consequence, has always enjoyed its immedi-ate favours at the expense of the true painter. Luckily ultimate rank is not settled by the popular voice, but by the accumulated judgment of trained minds ; and these have recognised (though not always so quickly as they might have done), that decorative excellence is an essential condition of artistic immortality. After a certain number of years, the star of the illustrator who lacks this excellence inevitably fades and dies; while that of the artist, which at first was obscure and dim, is taking place meanwhile among the great permanent lights.

For the painter himself the question has a secondary aspect, hardly less important than that which we have just discussed. Though Decoration must take precedence of Significance, Significance is the parent of Decoration. The outward attractive aspect of a picture is, in its essence, only the rhythmic fusion of the symbols which convey its inward meaning.

Decoration is thus no separate exterior quality which can be applied, like a varnish, to turn an illustration into a picture (though a thick varnish will sometimes make a bad picture less obtrusive), but a quality extracted by the painter from the particular subject-matter to hand, and therefore as infinitely varied as that subject-matter, except in so far as it is limited by conditions of material and function. Titian's *Bacchus and Ariadne*, Tintoret's *Milky Way*, Botticelli's *Mars and Venus*, Rubens' *Chateau de Stein*, Rembrandt's *Nativity*, Van Dyck's *Charles I.*, Vermeer's *Lady at a Spinet*, Reynolds' *Lord Heathfield*, and Turner's *Rain, Steam and Speed*, are all decorative ; but the decorative quality in each of them is a quality fitting that picture alone, arising naturally out of the particular thoughts and things with which it deals, and incapable of being transferred wholesale and applied to some other subject.

Rules and principles of decorative composition can thus never do more than suggest analogies between the artist's thoughts and the symbols appropriate for their expression. To construct and to elaborate definite canons of picture-making from the examples of former masters, as the older writers on art sometimes attempted to do, is to court failure. Identity of construction implies identity of thought, and the practice of fitting one man's thoughts into another man's picture schemes is responsible for a considerable proportion of the bad paintings with which Europe is lumbered.

It has been my aim in these pages to suggest so far as lay in my power, the directions in which the painter may profitably study this correspondence between thought and expression, so that from the infinite variety of devices and materials at his disposal, he may be able to select just those which are appropriate to his immediate purpose. If anywhere the accidental turn of a phrase should seem to suggest that there is some rigid formula or system by which all subjects may be made into good pictures, I trust what I have said here will prove that the suggestion was unintentional.

Yet there is one part of painting where it is possible that time and experience may effect a general improvement, and that is in matter of colour. Good colour is at once the most important factor in decorative effect, and the quality which trained painters most frequently fail to attain. When we think how we esteem even third-rate primitive masters who have produced good colour above the strong, learned and accomplished academic painters of later times who were not colourists, we may wonder that the attention of students has not been directed to colour far more seriously than is usually the case in art schools. The difficulty attending its use in connection with strong relief ought, in particular, to have been recognised and analysed long ago. The advantage too, of using only a limited number of colours in any single design, in spite of Whistler's precept and example, is still rarely insisted upon.

The great problem in connection with the subject-matter of painting is the relation of art to nature. "Truth to Nature," as we have seen, is one of those phrases which people are apt to use as if it were an infallible touchstone for works of art, without considering for a moment that, had this been so absolutely, the great masters would not be great, and the best works of art would be those which most nearly resembled our modern colour photography. Even the realist begins by using a convention or a symbol, instead of an exact imitation, for the lights and shadows which are beyond the scope of his medium; and so differs from the most arbitrary idealist only in the number and character of the symbols he employs. What degree of freedom, then, may be permitted to the artist in employing pictorial symbols to represent natural appearances ?

A few points at least seem clear. First we must observe the condition of Unity. All the symbols employed in a single work should be of the same kind and have the same relation to nature. If some are realistic all should be realistic; if some are capricious all should be capricious. The condition of Vitality next involves the emphasis in each symbol of the living forces, the vital character, of the thing represented, in preference to mere surface qualities. This effect of vitality will be enhanced if the symbol states no more than the essential features, if it states them clearly, and if it states them swiftly, for the very swiftness of the execution will convey a sense of power and liveliness to the spectator. This vitality must also be accompanied with the tenderness and subtlety born of long and earnest insight into nature, or the symbol, though spirited, will be shallow ; while the condition of Repose involves that the symbol shall take its place quietly in the work for which it has been designed.

Vitality and Infinity are thus the two pictorial conditions which bear directly upon the painter's treatment of nature. The one insists that he shall not regard nature as a dead thing, as an inert mass of brute matter, but as a collection of living organisms, much as modern science now teaches us to regard it. The other insists that he shall have an eye for the delicacy, refinements and complexity of natural forms and colours. So long therefore as the painter's symbols breathe that living force, and acknowledge that subtle tenderness, they will possess the essential character of nature, and be true to nature, whatever facts, or details, or appearances, they may, for pictorial reasons have to sacrifice.

In connection with this point, two other terms frequently used in art criticism may be discussed— Values and Finish. The discovery that natural appearances could be imitated in paint, by carefully matching their broad relations of tone, their "values," is often supposed to be a modern one, although every good painter since the Renaissance has understood the principle, and employed it as a matter of course in his work. In more recent times it has been elevated almost to the rank of a recipe for producing pictures; but the inquiry we have just been making will reveal its limitations. In a mere broad mosaic of tone values it is evident that neither the vital qualities nor the refinement of nature can be emphasised; we may have

U

a general resemblance to nature, but however effective, it will be a coarse, empty, and lifeless resemblance.

The principle may unquestionably be useful as a means of training students to grasp the general aspect of things, as part of their artistic alphabet; but it is no more a complete solution of artistic problems than a knowledge of the alphabet is a complete equipment for a poet. If Velasquez, who is sometimes named as the great master of values, depended for his reputation upon values alone, he might rank lower than the shadowy Mazo. It is because he could paint the living soul and the princely refinement of his sitters, and could fuse that life and subtlety into superbly decorative canvases, that his name stands high—not because he matched values with conspicuous taste.

The question of Finish is more troublesome.* Ruskin has described finish as " added fact," thereby epitomising the popular view. But, as we have seen, the condition of Vitality involves clear statement of living character, and this clearness of statement will frequently be obscured if we load it with too many details. All painters know that it is frequently impossible to retain in a finished picture the freshness and spirit of a rapid sketch. Up to a certain point finish is clearly necessary, if only that the pictorial symbol may be understood; after that point every

* Here, as elsewhere, Mr. Roger Fry's edition of " Reynolds' Discourses " (Seeley; 1905) has anticipated the conclusions reached.

added detail detracts from its first essential, Vitality, even though for a time it may enhance the sister essential, Infinity. The question is, where must the painter stop ?

To that question there must be countless answers, corresponding to the endless variety of the painter's subject-matter. In an altar-piece by Van Eyck, exquisite minuteness of detail contributes largely to the spectator's pleasure; in the later work of Rembrandt absence of detail has the same effect.

It would seem as if the painter had to make, at the outset, a great decision : should his aim be clearness of impression, or should it be richness of content? If clearness of impression be the aim (as it appears to be with most moderns) he will consider just how much finish will be possible without impairing the vitality of his picture, and will try to refrain from adding more. If his aim be richness of content, finish and detail may be a necessity. The painter will then direct his efforts to retaining as much vitality as he can, either by fusing the details with the larger masses (Titian in this is unrivalled), or by executing them with the most lively precision, as Holbein and Millais (in his Pre-raphaelite time) succeeded in doing. This last method, in painting at least, is possible only for a supremely gifted draughtsman ; a less lofty standard of delicacy results in meticulous dulness. Perfect fusion of detail is hardly more easy : so that, on the whole, average talent would seem well advised to aim at clearness of impression, and to avoid emptiness by working on a modest scale, with every available refinement of brush-work, pigment and colour.

The mistake of many moderns who aim at this clearness of expression is to imagine that it is sufficient in itself to make a good picture. They forget that the great masters who, like Gainsborough, have worked with a broad loose touch, avoid the fault of emptiness only by the infinite subtlety and gradation of their chiaroscuro and their colouring. Yet even if a painter working on these lines does sometimes incur the charge of emptiness (usually from making the picture larger than the contents warrant), he may still retain freshness of feeling and fine decorative quality; whereas a painter who works in the minute style, and does so imperfectly, commits artistic suicide. Decorative charm and liveliness of impression will alike be buried under a mass of tedious detail, and what was intended to be art will end as illustration, and dull illustration too. Official English painting is peculiarly liable to failure in this matter, as the corresponding work in France and Germany is often open to criticism on the count of emptiness. The Impressionists were wiser, and generally avoided working on large canvases.

In reviewing the aims and ideals of the painter we need dwell only upon one aspect of them—namely, the condition that they shall be the outcome of *personal* experience. We saw that the Narrative painter tries to render some aspect of nature as closely as his materials will admit, while the Satiric, Lyrical, Dramatic, and Despotic painters do not. Of that aspect they may select only those parts which are essential to their respective purposes, and reject all the rest. All painters except Narrative painters thus produce their effects not by attempting to paint the whole of nature, but by the emphatic rendering of some part or phase of nature —the choice of the part of nature to be emphasized being the business of the painter's personality.

The general limits of that choice are set by the class of art which the painter elects to follow, by the particular feeling he wishes to express, by the direction in which his taste and inclinations lie, and by one other strict condition, namely, that the part of nature chosen shall not correspond exactly or very closely with that chosen by any preceding painter. Only when learning his profession may the student, for the sake of experience, follow closely in the track of some earlier master, and try, for the nonce, to see with another's eyes, and to judge with another's taste.

Such originality for a time will invite the neglect or dislike of the public. The popular standard of perfection in the arts, being always set by past achievement, is a useless test for new genius. This last the crowd invariably receives with hesitation, if not with actual hostility, and the novel standard of taste and excellence which every artist creates is thus rarely accepted until it has been abused as incompetence or ugliness. The man who conforms to the standard of taste set by his age must inevitably be a second-rate artist, though he will probably be a popular painter. Those who wish to be more than that must recognize the necessity of being personal, of seeing with their own eyes, of thinking with their own minds, of delivering some message that is unquestionably theirs alone. The mechanical part of painting can only be learned with the help of the example of others; its subject-matter, on the other hand, must be chosen anew by each successive painter, with the certainty that, if just the same choice has ever been made before, its treatment will be labour in vain.

Finally I may return once more to the description of a good picture as "Personal Experience Emphasized by Emotion in terms of Decoration," to lay stress on the fact that neither Personality nor Experience nor Emotion nor Decoration nor Emphasis are sufficient by themselves. It is only in their perfect fusion that the solution of the problem of painting can be found, and to master the secret of this fusion is the hardest task of all. The greatest artists have had to sacrifice years of thought and labour in its pursuit: the pictures in which it has been attained beyond all reasonable challenge are rightly termed supreme masterpieces. In these works significance and decoration, thought and expression, matter and form, already noble in themselves, are so completely and indissolubly blended that we cannot think of the one without the other, and their harmonious unity is at once the stimulus and the despair of those who would travel on the same road.

To test and confirm the separate parts of our practice is perhaps humdrum work, for it is no more than a first preliminary stage in the journey to this distant ideal ; but until some royal road is invented it is still a necessary stage. In the attempt to make a rough and tentative map of the beginning of this route my notes may often be obscure, as they are certainly clumsy and incomplete. Yet I believe the larger landmarks are not far from their proper places, and my purpose will be served if, by their help, the reader can gain a general idea of the path along which every true artist must advance, and of the goal which lies, alas how far away! at the end of it.

SUMMARY

THE PAINTER

PERSONALITY

All great art being emphatically personal, is accompanied by variation from previously existing standards of excellence (pp. xviii, xix, 273, 277, 298, 309).

This personal variation is marked by a new intensity of feeling, by a new sense of vitality, and by a new rhythm of pattern (pp. 275, 276, 310, 311).

All great artists are pioneers, possessing these characteristics. In their followers, the second-rate artists, we find less intensity of feeling, less vitality and a feebler rhythmical sense (pp. 5-7, 282, 283).

EMOTION

Emotion is the keystone of painting as it is of poetry. What is not strongly felt is no material for the artist. The painter's emotion sums up and concentrates his experiences (imaginative or visual) in terms of rhythmical paint, as the poet's does in terms of rhythmical words (pp. 9-12, 65-68).

THEORY

Theory is not a substitute for talent, but its necessary teacher. Principles of design are not rigid moulds into which the subject-matter of a work has to be squeezed. Their task is to suggest to the artist the particular means by which each given subject can be perfectly expressed (pp. 18–24, 301, 302).

TRADITION

Tradition is no more than the body of principles which secure conformity between art and its contemporary environment. What is a perfect tradition for one period or climate may thus be a fatal influence in another period or climate, because it does not fit the changed conditions. Hence the danger of revivals of old methods (pp. **xxi-xxiii**).

TRAINING

Systems of art teaching have commonly failed from not recognising the necessity of progress— from enslavement to a fixed canon of ideal beauty. No such fixed canon of ideal beauty can be set up as a standard for future achievement. We cannot do again what has already been done by a great artist : we must do something different. Each field of artistic activity is exhausted by the first great artist who gathers a full harvest from it (pp. xiii-xxii, 68, 272, 277, 291, 292).

The great artists of the Renaissance were born into an imperfect tradition ; to make progress they had only to carry this forward towards perfection. Modern artists, of whom Rembrandt is the greatest, inherit a complete tradition, from which no direct advance is possible. Thus they have first to go back to more primitive conditions, to secure intense vitality and emphatic rhythm of pattern, and from this base to start a fresh advance. A period of incessant experiment succeeds, and this usually terminates in the search for a pictorial atmosphere in which the various elements of the design may be harmoniously fused and united (pp. 266–280, 293–298).

AIMS AND IDEALS

The painter's ideals may be conveniently classified in relation to the development of the human race.

I. *Primitive Art*, which is characterised by intense enjoyment of rhythm and pattern, and by emphatic statement of vitality (pp. 241, 242, 275–277).

II. *Despotic Art*, which celebrates the triumphs of rulers, races, or religions. It is usually imposing in scale, severe in treatment, with firm contours, and flat, simple colouring. Details, accessories and strong shadows are avoided. Its character may sometimes be transmitted to minor forms of art with conspicuous success (pp. 243–247).

III. *Individual Art*, a more direct product of the artist's personality, divides naturally into four sections :

(i) Dramatic Painting: the art of a crisis.
It suggests the conflict of opposing forces by marked contrasts of rhythm and tone and colour. If the dramatic sense be lacking a painting may be ineffective; yet contrasts must be used with restraint, or the result is melodrama (pp. 248–252).

(ii) Lyrical Painting: the art of a mood.
Its essentially contemplative character is emphasised by the harmony and gentle fusion of tones, colours and contours ; by the suggestion of repose or of slow movement. In its perfection it demands a sensitiveness of touch and of taste which are found only with great technicians (pp. 252–255).

(iii) Satiric Painting : the art of ridicule.
It seems to depend chiefly upon the lively use

of line; an elaborate technique commonly detracts from its effectiveness. It permits almost unbounded license in treatment (pp. 255–257).

(iv) Narrative Painting : the art of description. Though its apparent standard of literal imitation, or exact statement, is still popular as providing a convenient critical formula, realism can only be employed safely within narrow limits. It becomes a source of danger the moment it conflicts with the decorative aspect of a picture. Narrative painting is thus less valuable in itself than as a remedy for mannerism ; it is a splendid tonic but an intolerable diet (pp. 39–41, 257–263, 303–305, 309).

The peril of working exclusively from nature : the value of memory (pp. 26–30).

THE PICTURE

SUBJECT AND TREATMENT

A good picture is a decorative panel, which conveys its message to us primarily by the visible attractiveness of its pattern. Its outward decorative aspect has thus a definite precedence over its subject-matter—its inward significance. Where Decoration is overwhelmed by Significance we have an Illustration, not a Picture. Decoration without Significance still leaves us a noble pattern; Significance without Decoration leaves us a mere diagram (pp. 299–300).

Yet Significance is the parent of Decoration. The decorative aspect of any picture is a quality extracted from the subject-matter to hand; a quality fitting that picture alone, and incapable of being

transferred to another subject. This adjustment
of subject-matter and treatment is effected by
Design, which may be described as Emphasis subject
to Pictorial Conditions (pp. 24, 35, 36, 301–302).

EMPHASIS

Pictorial emphasis is the expression of the painter's
emotion. He accentuates thereby just those points
in his message which deserve accent, through the
symbols, the plan, the spacing, the shadow, the
colour and the materials which he chooses for his
work (pp. 9–12, 15, 36, 37).

PICTORIAL CONDITIONS

There are four conditions to which this choice
must conform, four qualities which all fine pictures
in some degree possess:

I. *Unity*

A picture must be complete in itself, a panel with
a single purpose. If two or more groups or masses
divide the spectator's interest the result is imperfect (p. 33).

This unity is controlled by the major rhythm of
the design. All decorative quality depends upon
the presence of this rhythmic element, which involves a repetition or balancing of the dominant
contours, tones, and colours, as metrical stress is
repeated or balanced in a poem. If this rhythmic
element be absent the contours, tones and colours
will not make an attractive pattern; the work will
in consequence be undecorative, will cease to be a
picture, and will become an illustration (p. 38 *note;*
pp. 64–68).

Unity of Symbol (pp. 41–44, 304); of Plan (pp
61–64); of Spacing (pp. 79–81); of Recession
(pp. 87–90); of Shadow (pp. 96–100); of Colour,
(pp. 115–122).

II. *Vitality*

A picture must suggest the vitality which pervades all nature, not mere surface appearances, or it will be cold, inert and dead (pp. 33–34).

The study of values alone is thus insufficient (pp. 305–306).

The subordinate rhythms in a painting assist in conveying this sense of life (p. 38 *note;* pp. 66–67).

The immense importance of Vitality in Primitive Art (p. 242), and in Modern Art (pp. 275–276, 293, 294).

Vitality of Symbol (pp. 44–55, 304–307); of Plan (pp. 64–71); of Spacing (pp. 81–83); of Recession (pp. 90–91); of Shadow (pp. 101–103); of Colour (pp. 122–126).

III. *Infinity*

A picture must convey a suggestion of mystery, of evanescence, of refinements which the eye cannot precisely measure, or it will be hard and empty (p. 34).

Infinity of Symbol (pp. 55–58, 304–308); of Plan (pp. 71–72); of Spacing (pp. 83–85); of Recession (pp. 91–94); of Shadow (pp. 103–106); of Colour (pp. 126–129).

IV. *Repose*

A picture is a decorative panel, which must take its place on a wall quietly, or it will be obtrusive and vulgar (p. 35).

Repose of Symbol (pp. 58–59); of Plan (pp. 72–76); of Spacing (pp. 85–86); of Recession (p. 94); of Shadow (pp. 107–108), of Colour (pp. 129–134).

ART AND NATURE

Nature is the painter's storehouse (pp. 25–30).

Yet painting is not a literal imitation of nature ; the materials and purpose of a picture set limits to imitation. We can suggest nature only by painted symbols (pp. 39–59, 241–242, 257–263).

Vitality and Infinity are the two qualities which the pictorial symbol must retain at all costs (pp. 303–305). Vitality is most effectively conveyed by the emphasis of a few significant features (pp. 44–55, 293–295).

The difficulty problem of Finish. The painter must decide at the outset whether his aim is to be clearness of impression or richness of content. Clearness of impression is the simpler and safer of the two ideals (pp. 307–308).

INDEX OF ARTISTS

Printed in Great Britain by Butler & Tanner, *Frome and London*

Lightning Source UK Ltd.
Milton Keynes UK
UKHW020642180421
382202UK00002B/23